MONUMENT AVENUE

MONUMENT AVENUE

BRIAN ROSE

CIRCA

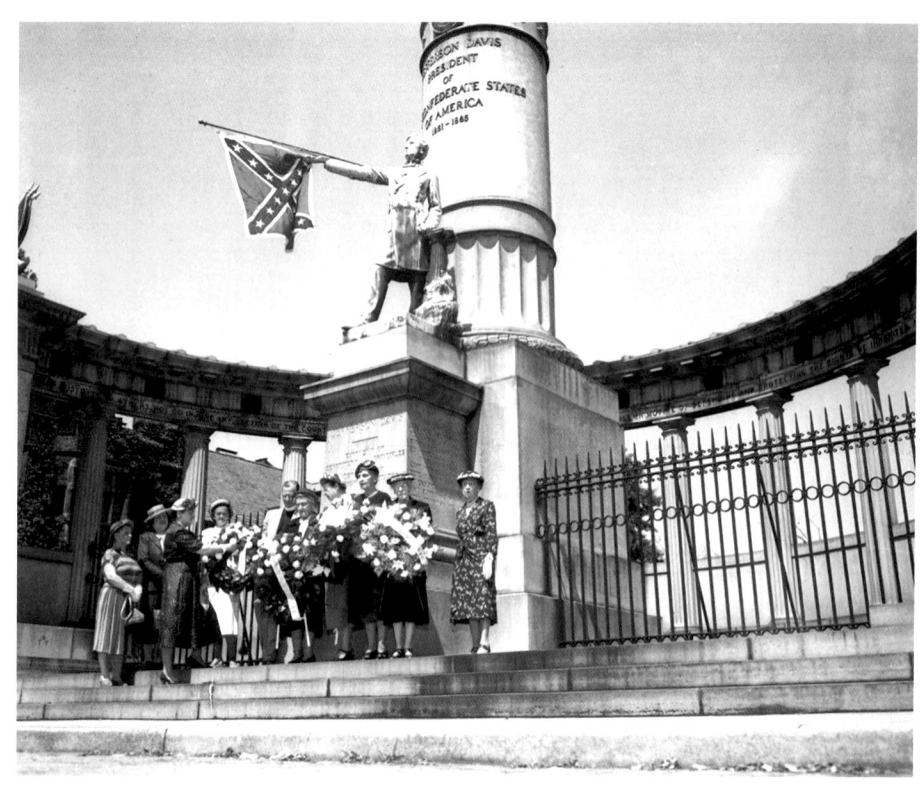

ANNUAL MEMORIAL SERVICE OF THE UNITED DAUGHTERS OF THE CONFEDERACY AT THE JEFFERSON DAVIS MEMORIAL, JUNE 1952

VIRGINIA ROOTS
BRIAN ROSE

I am a New Yorker, a self-identification that presupposes the likelihood that one may have come from somewhere else, from another state, or from anywhere in the world. My work as a photographer and musician emerged from the rubble and creative ferment of New York City in the late '70s and early '80s. But I was born and raised in Tidewater, Virginia, a place steeped in history, where English settlers in 1607 established a colony on the swampy shore of the James River, and the place where Africans first arrived on a Dutch ship as human chattel in 1619. The British surrender at Yorktown, twelve miles from where my family lived, effectively ended the Revolutionary War, and after the Civil War, Jefferson Davis, the president of the Confederacy, was imprisoned at nearby Fort Monroe, where my father worked at the end of his career with the Army.

While it is possible to live in Virginia and remain relatively untouched by the existence of this powerful and ubiquitous backstory, that was certainly not the case for me. My family lived in Williamsburg, the former colonial capital, now a tourist destination, and as a child, the restored area with its manicured streets and gardens was my playground. It was a carefully buffed recreation of the eighteenth century suspended between reality and imagination, between document and myth. Ada Louise Huxtable, the architecture critic, once wrote: 'What the perfect fake or impeccable restoration lacks are the hallmarks of time and place. They deny imperfections, alterations, and accommodations; they wipe out all the incidents of life and change.'

This ephemeral world – of neither here nor there – was, however, the actual location of my upbringing. I joined the fife and drum corps at nine years old, wore a costume with a three-cornered hat, and performed for thousands of visitors as well as two presidents of the United States. I attended church services with my father at Bruton Parish Church and was present at the noteworthy, but dimly remembered moment when Lyndon Johnson was challenged from the pulpit by our minister, who called into question the president's Vietnam policy. And when Nixon came to town for a conference, the fife and drum corps played patriotic tunes while protesters heckled from across the street. The church with its original eighteenth-century bell tower sat directly next door to the distinguished brick home of George Wythe, signatory of the Declaration of Independence, and friend and mentor of Thomas Jefferson. Past and present were, improbably melded together, all of a piece. Yes, Williamsburg occupies a surreal performative space, but I came to understand that the kind of authenticity Huxtable pined for was, perhaps, a dubious concept in the meta-reality of modern America.

Williamsburg, both the restoration and the present-day town, is dominated by its colonial-era trappings, but the Civil War's lingering presence is never far away. There were earthen fortifications in the woods behind my house, weathered trenches, and I once found a metal uniform button hidden in the dirt. Richmond, the state and former Confederate capital, is only an hour up Route 5, a scenic two-lane highway that parallels the James River with its gracious tobacco plantations dating back to the seventeenth and eighteenth centuries. Richmond, during my youth, was a city struggling to preserve its image as a genteel Southern capital. Middle-class whites were fleeing to the suburbs leaving an increasingly Black inner city, the cigarette companies had moved their plants out of town, and newly built freeways slashed through old neighbourhoods and snaked through the industrial riverfront downtown. But the statues of Confederate generals loomed undisturbed on their pedestals along Monument Avenue, and the good old boys' network carried on in the Jefferson Hotel and the Commonwealth Club. The South may have lost the war, but the honour of Robert E. Lee, the patron saint of the Lost Cause, remained undisputed.

Despite the penumbra of history I lived under in Virginia, I felt oddly disconnected from the past on a more intimate level. In short, I had no grandparents. My father's parents had died young, leaving him in the care of an elder sibling, and on my mother's side it was less clear what happened. It seems that she had fled an abusive home environment after graduating from high school aged sixteen, and never went back, never had any contact with her family. My father grew up on the south side of the James River, among farmers and merchants in a small town surrounded by peanut and cotton fields not far from the scene of Nat Turner's 1831 slave uprising. He once told me that as a child, he woke up in terror one night as a cross burned in their front yard. But he never provided any context for the story, any explanation for why they were targeted, apparently, by the Klan.

Quite simply, I could not place myself mentally or physically in that landscape. It did not have anything to do with me, or so I believed. My father, in his own way, rebelled by leaving home to attend the University of Virginia. He was the first Rose to go to college. When my father died, my sister and I scattered his ashes in Grays Creek, a small tributary of the James River. We understood instinctively that the James was the central element of his life. The journey he had made from one side of the river to the other was not far as the crow flies, but it represented a more profound journey of personal renewal from country to city, from the old South to the new. My mother, always strong-willed and fiercely independent, with a statuesque bearing that made her seem taller than she was, vaguely used to talk about coming from broken-down aristocracy – that it was all lost in the Great Depression she said – but there was no family to interact with, no one to confirm the story, and no homestead. I shrugged it off.

Over the years, I wondered about the history I never had, but I was determined to create a new identity for myself untethered to my Virginia roots. Like my father, I attended UVA, briefly studying urban design, and eventually graduated from New York's Cooper Union. After school, I pursued a career focused on the documentation of cultural and historical landscapes. Most notably, I photographed the Lower East Side, the famous immigrant neighbourhood of New York, and then in 1985 began photographing the Iron Curtain, the Berlin Wall, and the subsequent rebuilding of Berlin. In 2016, I responded to the unexpected and alarming election of Donald Trump by photographing Atlantic City with its ravaged streets and bankrupt casinos as a metaphor for America as a whole.

In the spring of 2020, the Covid-19 pandemic swept across the country, hitting New York especially hard, and the city was placed on lockdown by Governor Cuomo. In March and April, I wandered through the neighbourhood of Williamsburg, Brooklyn, its empty streets bare and frozen – as if time had stopped for my camera – keeping a safe distance from the few others who ventured out. I self-published a book called *Williamsburg Bkn: In Time of*

Plague, marketing it on Kickstarter. And I used the quarantine time at home to begin investigating my missing Virginia roots on various genealogy websites.

What I discovered left me dumbfounded. I peeled back the family's layers on my mother's side all the way to Jamestown – to the first supply ship that arrived in 1608, showing up just in time to save the few dozen colonists still alive but near starvation. One of my earliest ancestors may well have been present when Pocahontas and John Rolfe were married, an event that ended war with the Indians, and a few years later, when the census of 1624 was taken, was found living on a plantation called Jordan's Journey on the James River just south of Richmond. There were only 1,200 people of European descent in all of Virginia at that time. My later ancestors settled in Georgia and Mississippi – my fourth great-grandmother was a Creek Indian, and my third great-grandfather died in the battle of Vicksburg fighting for the South. For unknown reasons, my grandparents migrated to Washington, D.C., and then back to Virginia. My immediate family ultimately ended up in a suburban-style ranch house on the outskirts of Williamsburg, precisely four miles from the excavations of the original fort at Jamestown.

The Rose side of the family also traces its roots to Jamestown, to Surry County, directly across the river. My seventh great-grandfather, William Rose, settled in 1650 on the property adjacent to Smith's Fort, land given to John Rolfe and Pocahontas by Chief Powhatan, precisely at the spot on Grays Creek where my sister and I had scattered our father's ashes. It was as if we were all homing pigeons, somehow tuned to the way back, over centuries of time.

To a great extent, the revelation of this missing history was exhilarating, but it was distressing as well. These early Virginians were well-to-do planters, with much of their wealth derived from slave labour, not to mention that the land they claimed was essentially stolen from Native people. At the same time, however, these first Virginia families were the catalysts for American democracy, and they espoused the enlightenment ideals that underpin the Declaration of Independence and the Constitution, among the most remarkable achievements in Western civilisation.
I still regard Thomas Jefferson's UVA campus with its Roman Pantheon-inspired dome and classical colonnades as one

of the greatest works of architecture in North America, an audaciously conceived beacon of learning perched on the edge of the Appalachian wilderness. This epitome of American idealism was built, however, largely by enslaved labour, and a circular granite memorial echoing the nearby Rotunda now acknowledges this integral and sobering fact.

One of my great, great, great-grandfathers was awarded 486 acres of land by Jefferson in appreciation for his service in the Revolutionary War. He was also, like Jefferson, the owner of slaves. And most remarkable was the story of my third great-uncle, who departed the Tidewater region of Virginia, like a Faulkner character, to set up a sugar plantation in Louisiana. His plantation, known as Hard Times, was in 1850 the most prosperous in the Mississippi Delta, with as many as 350 enslaved labourers working the fields and operating the sugar mill. The Civil War brought ruin and an end to the plantation economy. It did not, of course, do away with the racism underlying American society both in the South and the North. Not by a long shot.

In New York, the Covid pandemic continued, but the city's crisis eased as people masked up and maintained social distancing. Donald Trump, unwilling to accept responsibility or listen to the advice of experts, recklessly encouraged Americans to shop, eat out and carry on as usual as the death toll from the virus mounted across the country. Then, on 25 May, George Floyd, a Black man living in Minneapolis, was killed by a white police officer while under arrest for allegedly passing a counterfeit $20 bill. The next day a mobile-phone video of Floyd's arrest was made public, the officer's knee pressing against his throat, his gasping, repeated last words, 'I can't breathe'. The video went viral, sending shockwaves through the body politic, shattering the preternatural calm of the pandemic's previous two months. Protesters took to the streets in Minneapolis and were met by tear gas and rubber bullets. Over the following weeks, millions throughout the U.S. marched against racism and police violence, and 'Black Lives Matter' became a rallying cry taken up by a diverse cross-section of the public.

In Richmond, demonstrations focused on Monument Avenue with its statues of generals and other Confederate luminaries. These stolid ghosts of the past were suddenly reanimated in the passion of the BLM movement, and the

longstanding debate surrounding these totems of the Confederacy – whether they should be removed or maintained with some sort of historic contextualisation – now appeared moot. In early July, it became clear that the end of the road was approaching for Monument Avenue. On 10 July, protesters pulled Jefferson Davis from his pedestal, and two days later, I drove down to Richmond to document the last days of the grand boulevard of the Lost Cause.

In travelling to Richmond, I should point out that I have not been a total stranger to my home state since moving to New York. Over the years, I made dozens of trips to visit my parents, rendezvoused there with my sister who flew in from San Francisco, and on several occasions marched down the Duke of Gloucester Street with the alumni of the Colonial Williamsburg Fifes and Drums. But this time, it felt different. I was on a mission to repossess, on my own terms, my birthright and heritage. It was not about atonement for a history I was not responsible for, but it was about seizing the moment when the past connected to the present in a circle of time, memory and place. It felt purposeful, conscious, and I could see arrayed before me a palimpsest of genetic code and geography, like a map, like personal destiny revealed.

As I stood on Monument Avenue in the low winter sun surveying the pedestals that once elevated J.E.B. Stuart and Stonewall Jackson above the crowd, and the brazenly, triumphantly, desecrated plinth of Robert E. Lee, I thought about how American democracy had nearly collapsed in a tawdry display of banner-waving, cult-like allegiance to a wannabe dictator, in a spasm of racial animus. Our better angels prevailed, just barely. We are left now with empty pedestals on Monument Avenue and a sense of loss. Not, of course, for the bronze idols promoted by the United Daughters of the Confederacy, not for the Lost Cause. And certainly, we can learn to accept, though not excuse, the imperfections of the Founding Fathers, men of their time, who arrived at Jamestown and sought to create a new world. But there is loss, nevertheless, for the pantheon of heroes we once revered, their icons now toppled or tarnished, and there is the corresponding loss of ideals displaced by voices of demagoguery and bigotry. We are left with empty pedestals on Monument Avenue as the sun comes up, and I point my car north on I-95 back home to New York City.

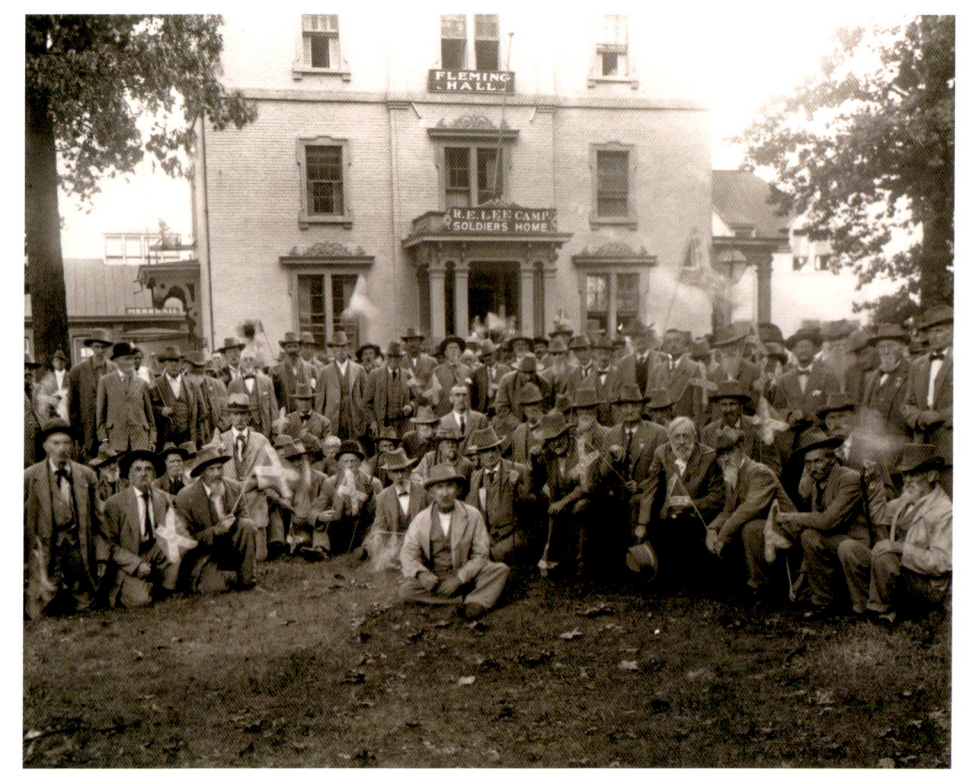

ROBERT E. LEE CAMP SOLDIERS' HOME, 1911, ON THE SITE NOW OCCUPIED BY THE UNITED DAUGHTERS OF THE CONFEDERACY MEMORIAL BUILDING

'THE PAST IS NEVER DEAD; IT'S NOT EVEN PAST.' — WILLIAM FAULKNER

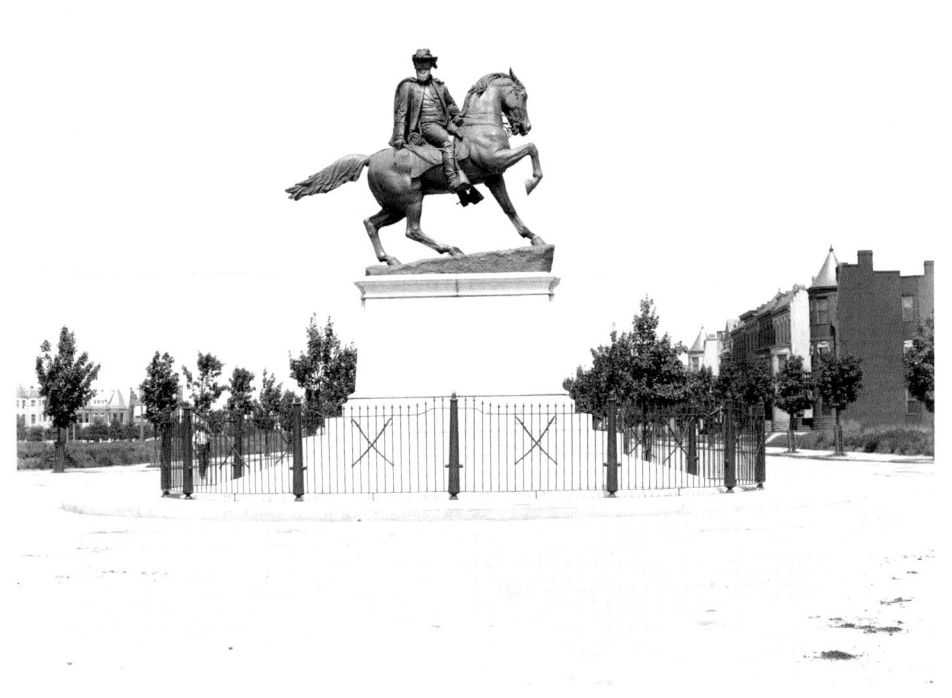

J.E.B. STUART MONUMENT, 1907

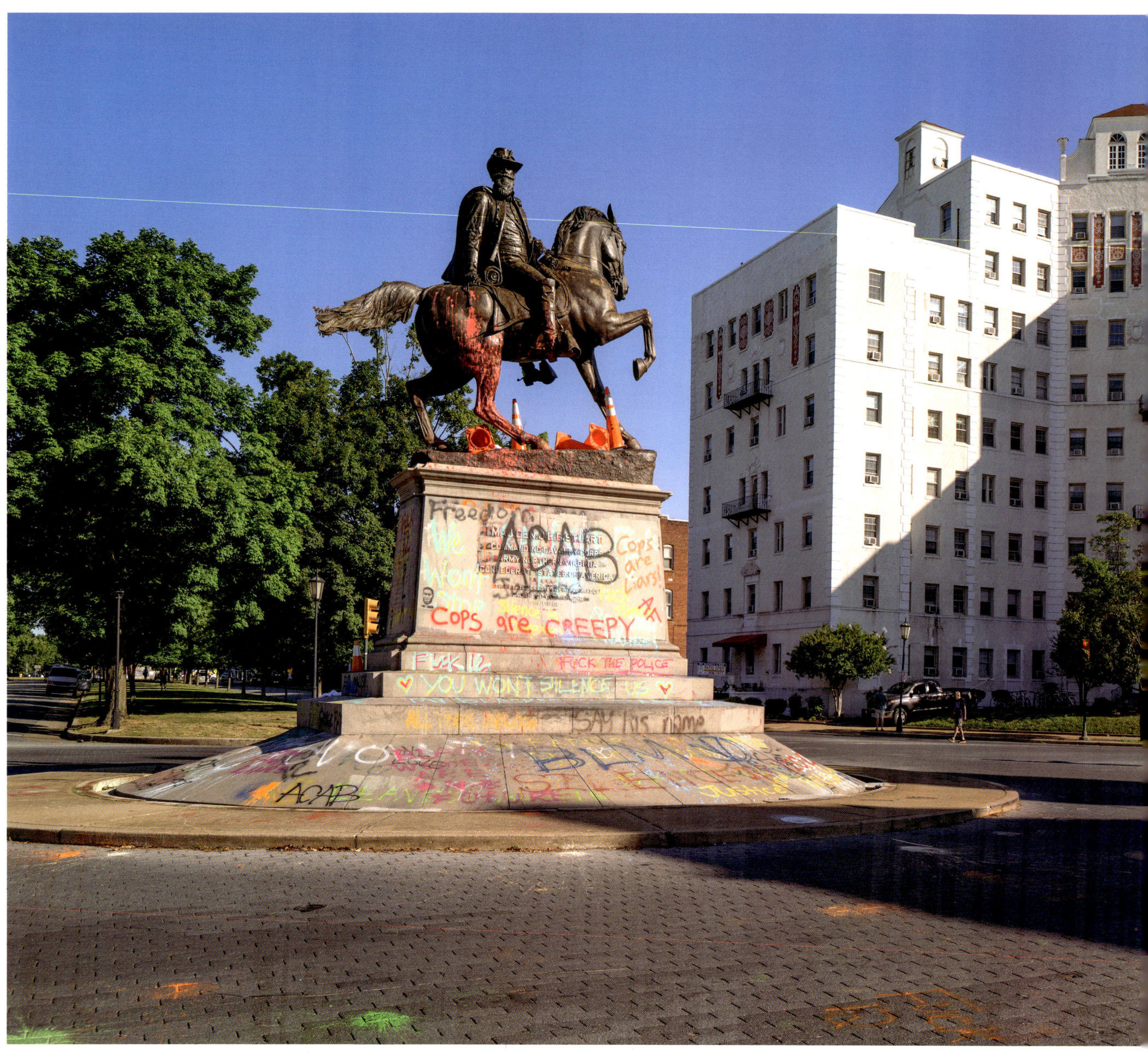

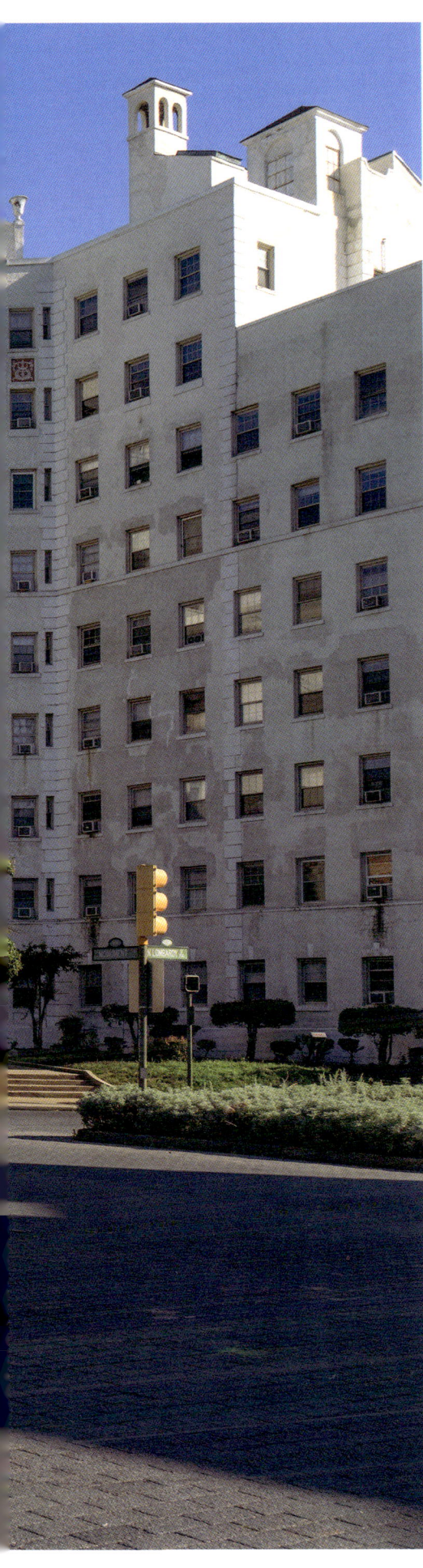

J.E.B. STUART

War, with its relentless fury, swept onward over every foot of Virginia soil. The enemy, in ever-increasing hosts, encompassed you about and sat down over against this devoted city – the Capital of the Confederacy – and within a twelve-month the bitter fate that had been averted from you by Stuart and his troopers, swiftly and suddenly descended upon you.

The days of our years of destruction and reconstruction have been many and full of sorrow, but today we behold a resurrection and ascension as marvelous as it is glorious. Your city is not only rebuilt, but it has expanded beyond imagination. Where we now stand was then open country. The triumphant march of progress has opened up this magnificent Monument Avenue, crowned as it is by the imposing statue of General Lee and the memorial to Jefferson Davis. Into this goodly company we come now to place the heroic statut of a man who, take him for all in all, we ne'er Shall look upon his like again.

Theodore Stanford Garnett
30 May 1907

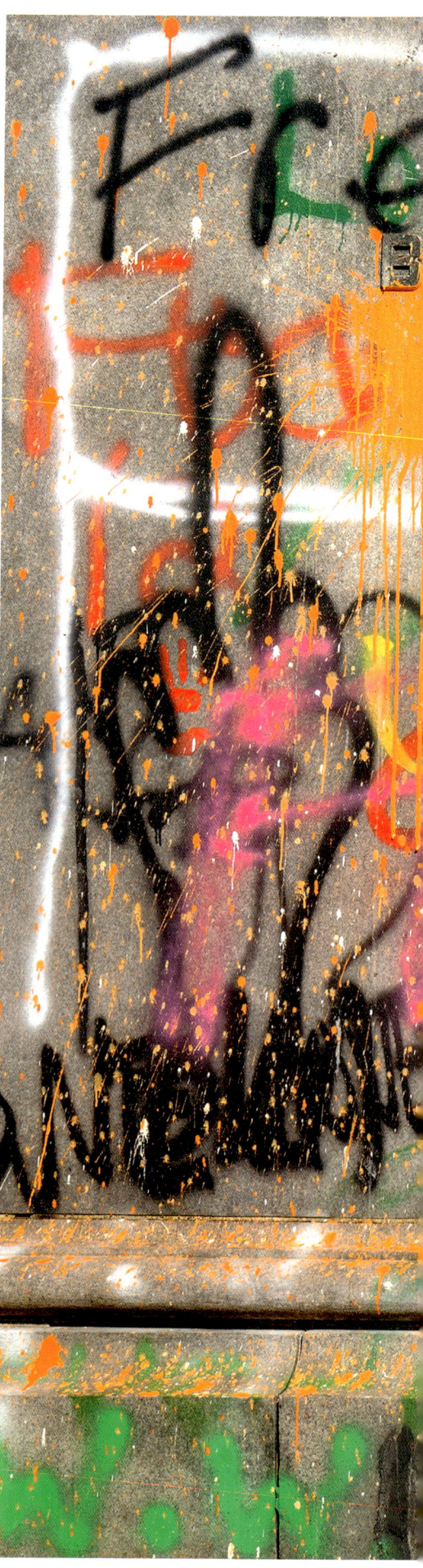

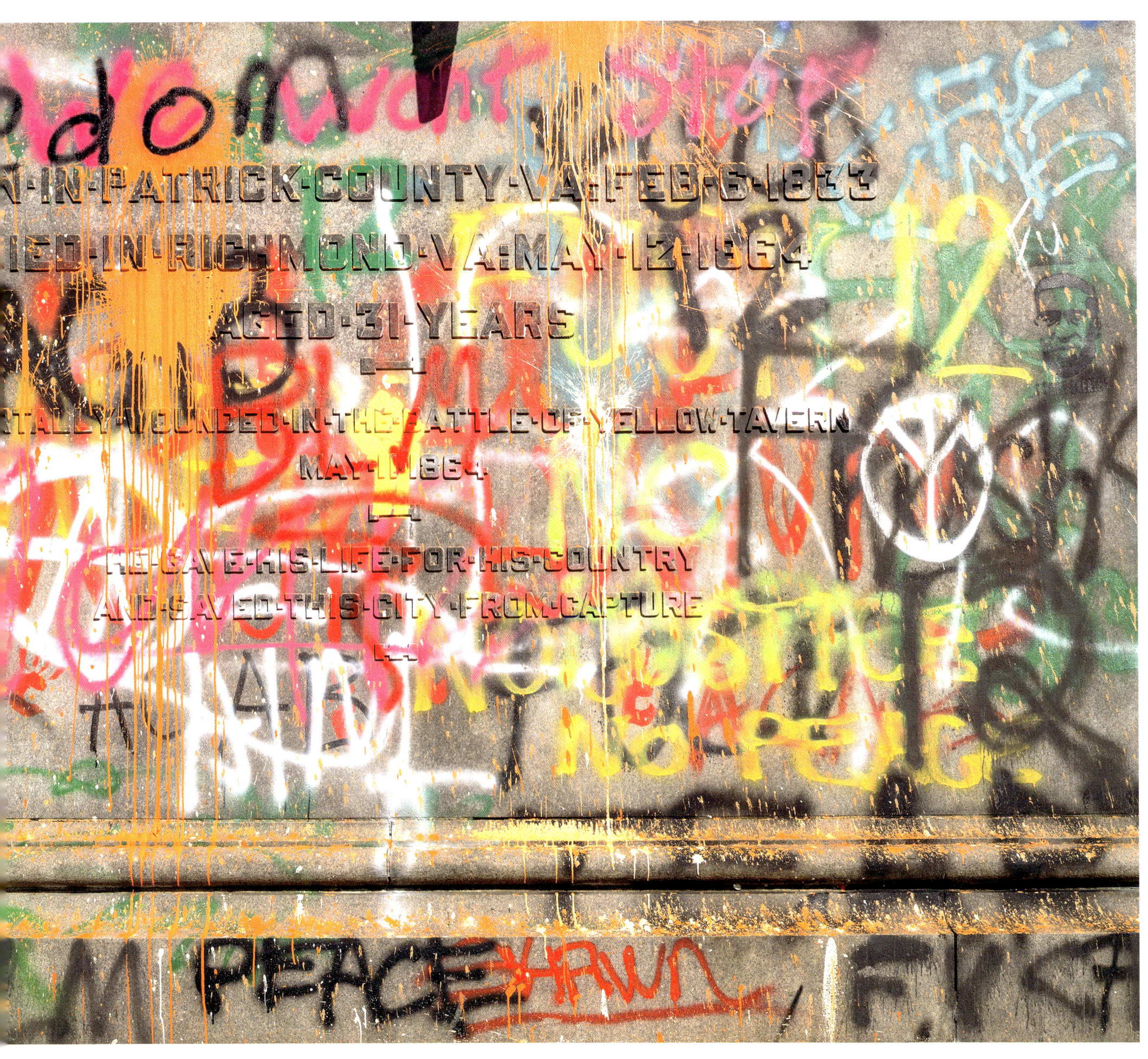

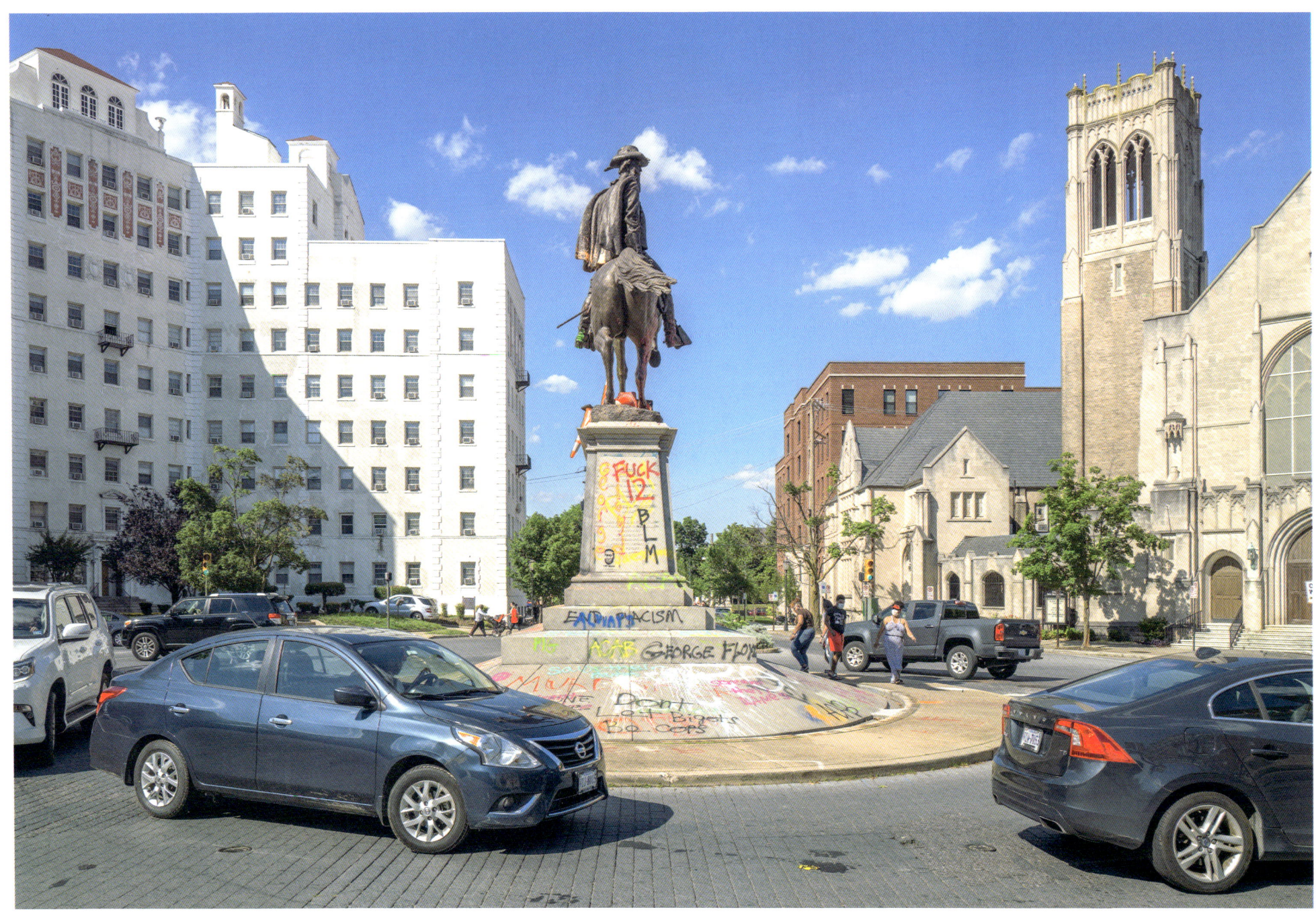

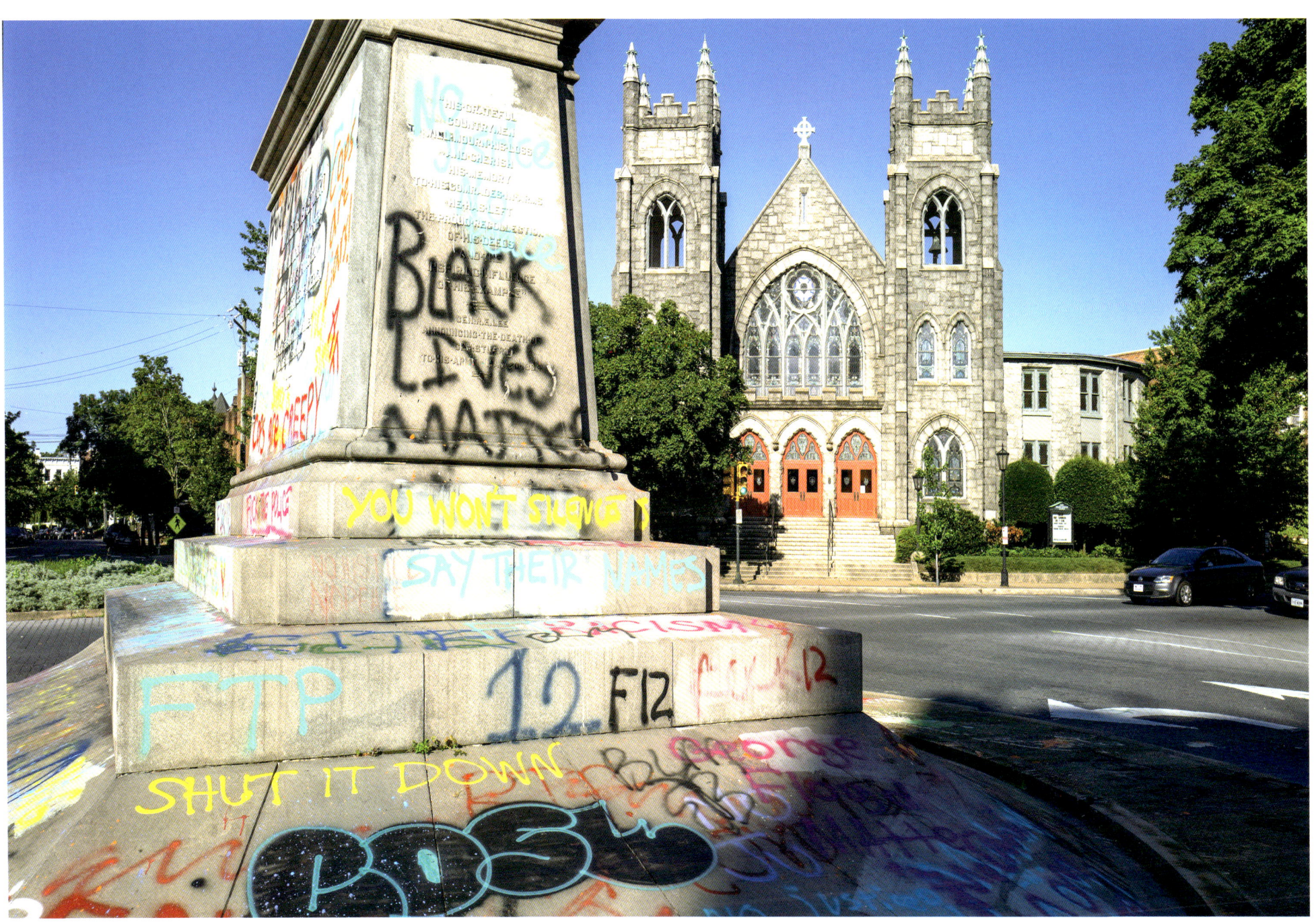

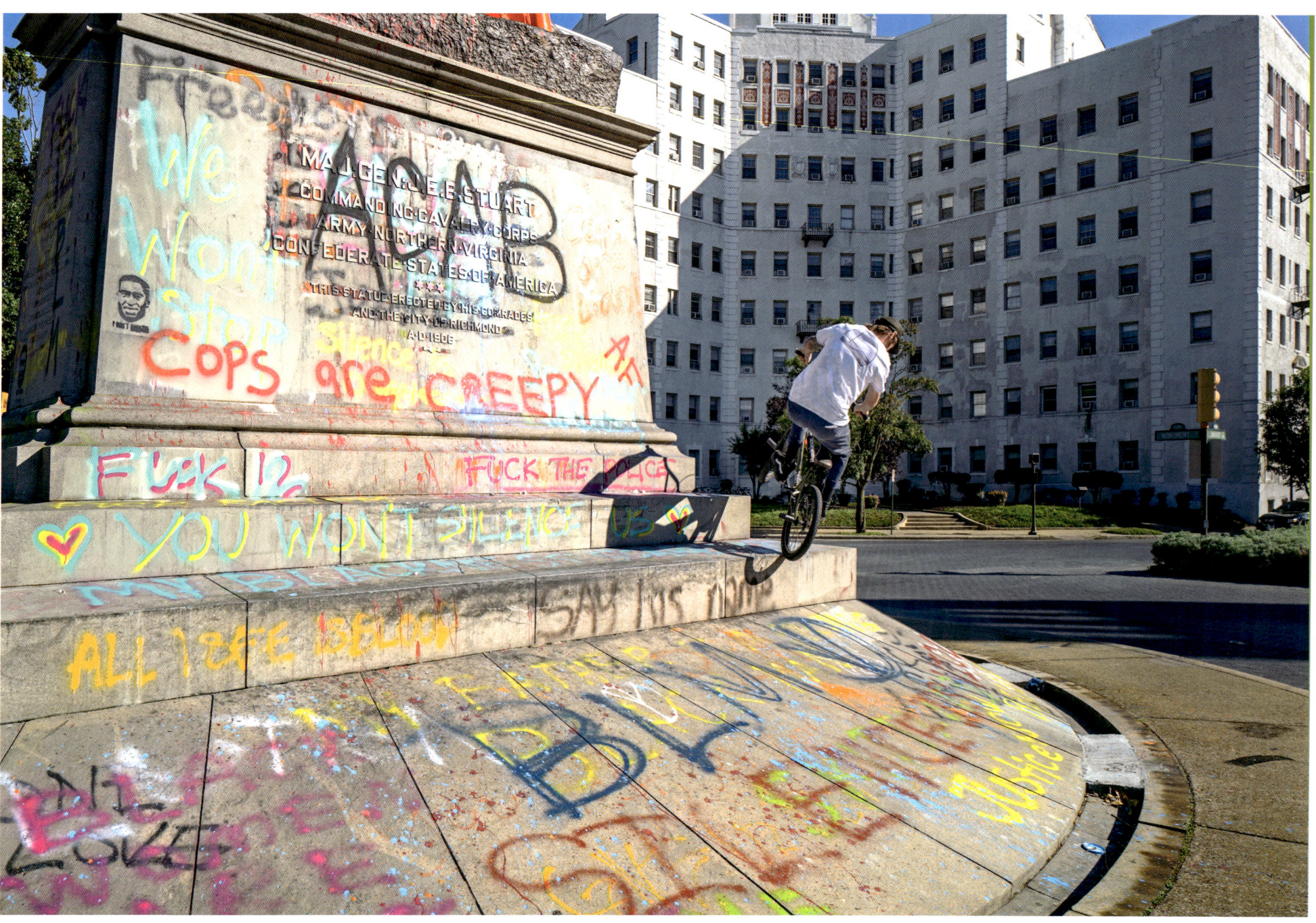

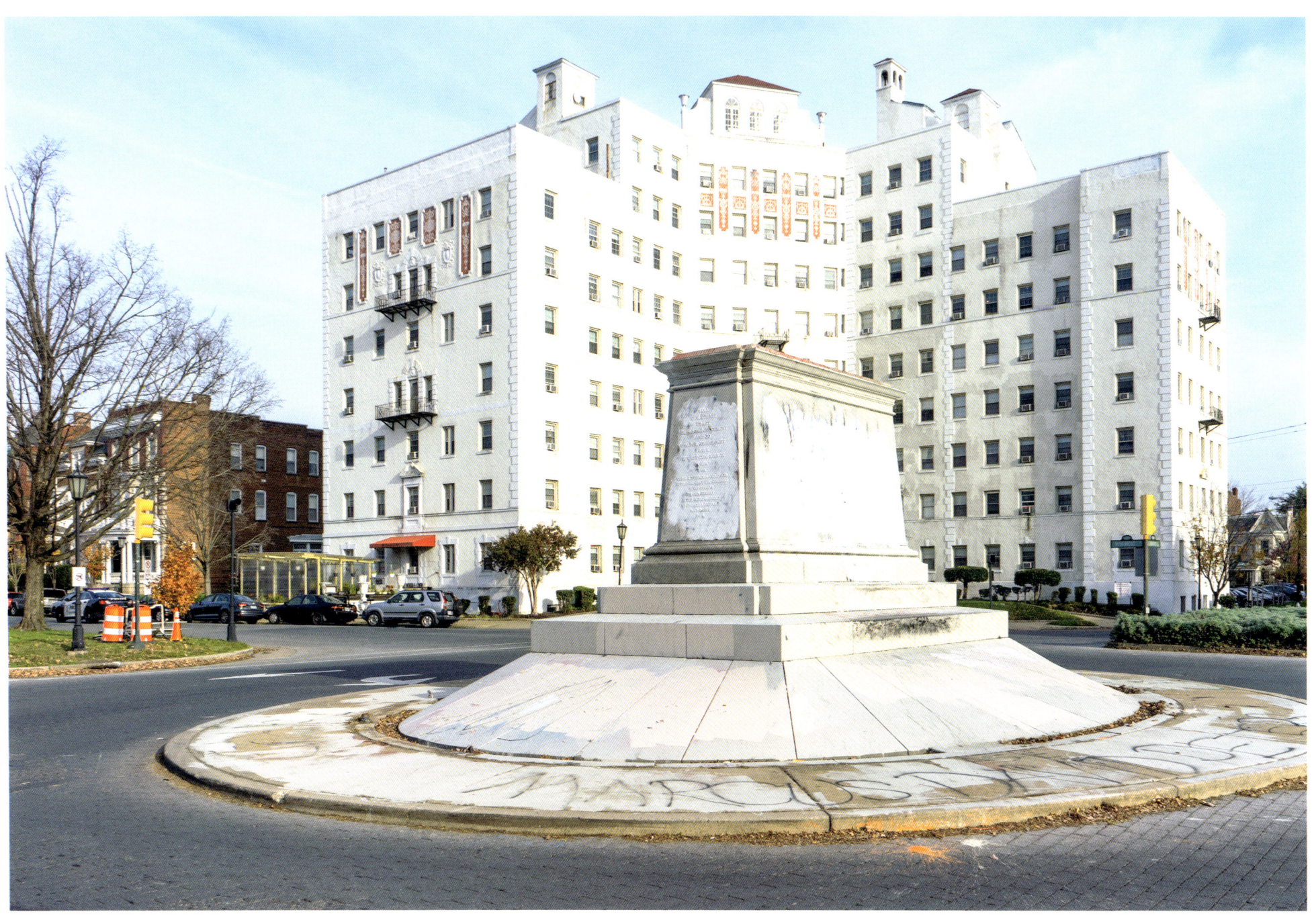

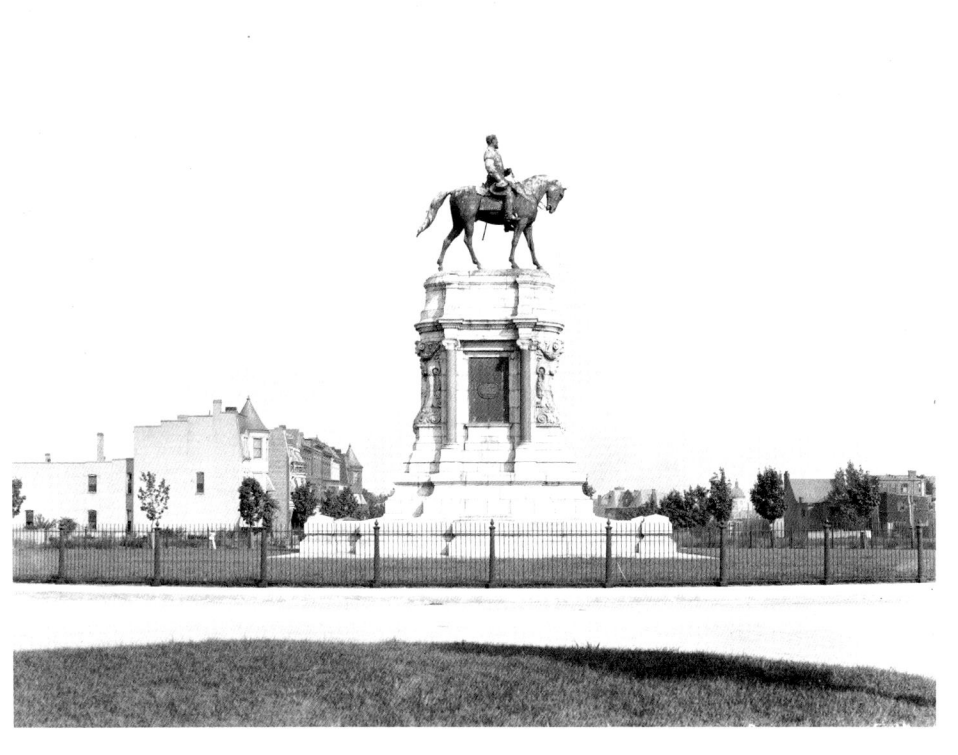

ROBERT E. LEE MONUMENT, 1890

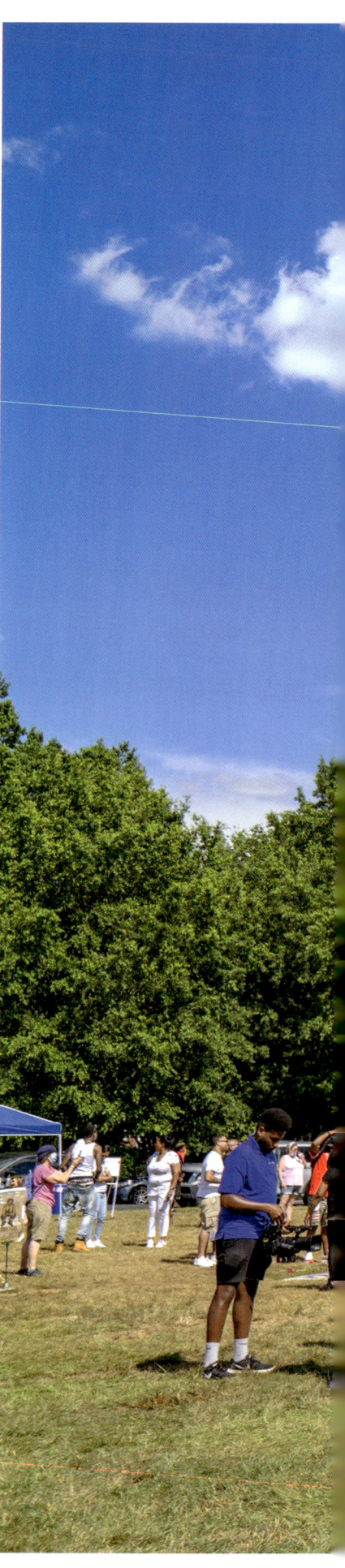

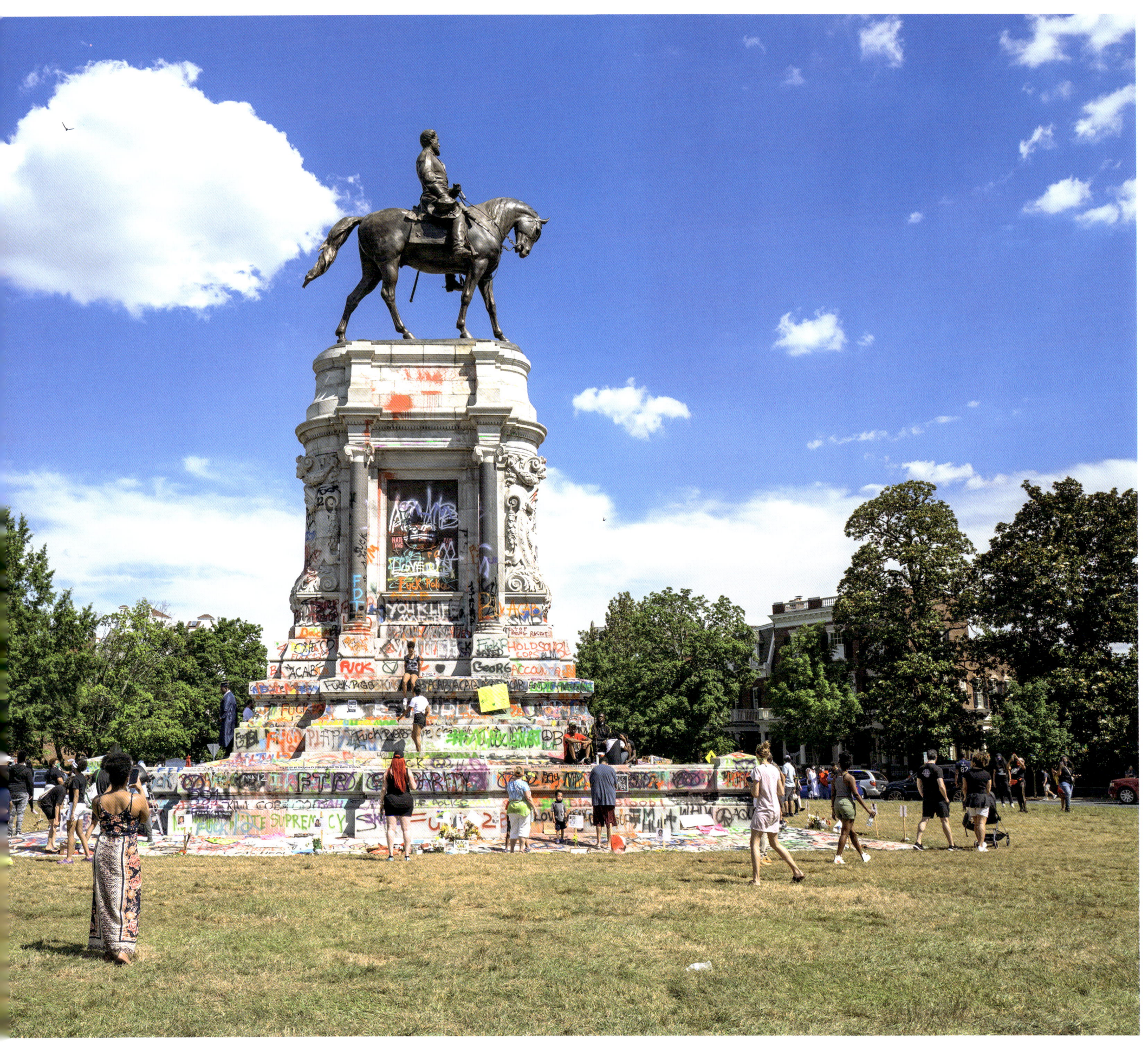

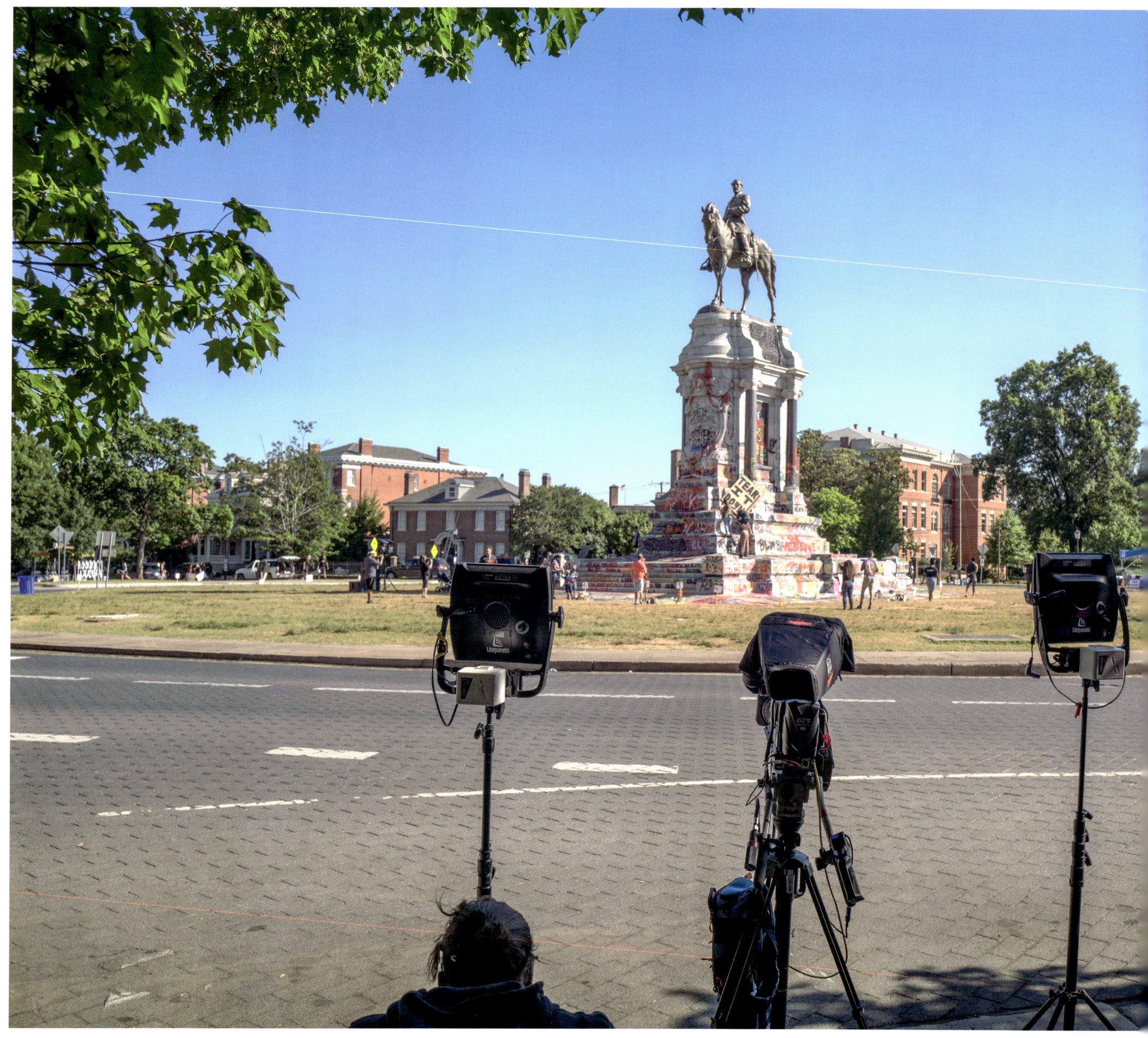

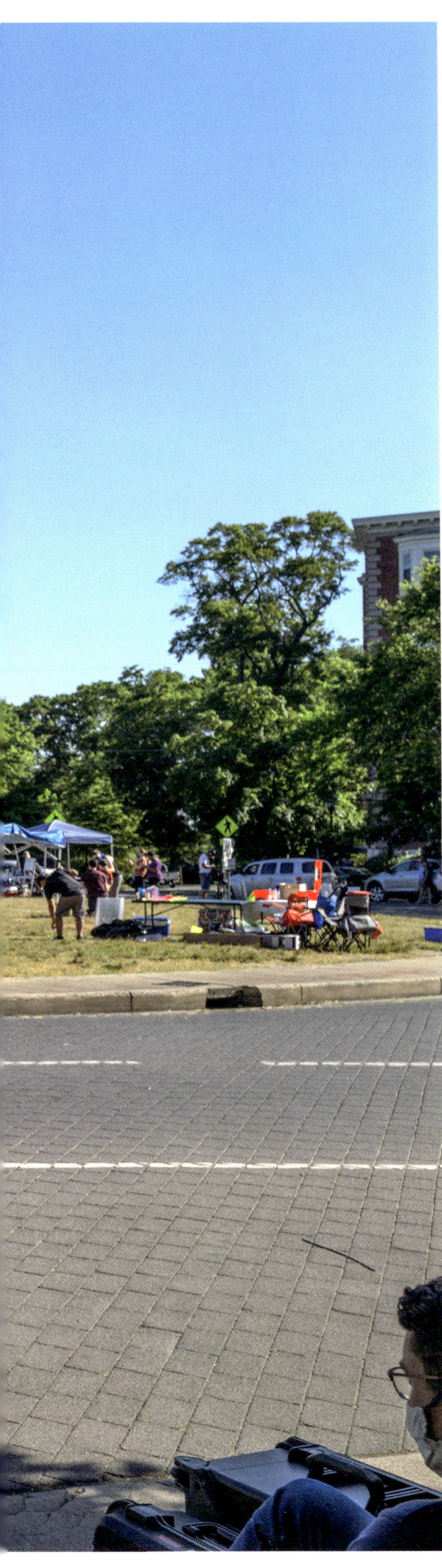

ROBERT E. LEE

Last Thursday, May 29th, on which the equestrian statue of General Robert E. Lee was unveiled in Richmond, marks an ever-memorable epoch in the history not only of that historic city and of Virginia, but of the whole South, for on that day was witnessed one of the grandest demonstrations of devoted love and affection ever shown for one of the grandest and noblest characters that ever lived in 'all the tide of time'. Such a universal and sincere, heartfelt tribute of honor and affection was never before given to any man, and he was eminently worthy of it.

Staunton Spectator, and General Advertiser
4 June 1890

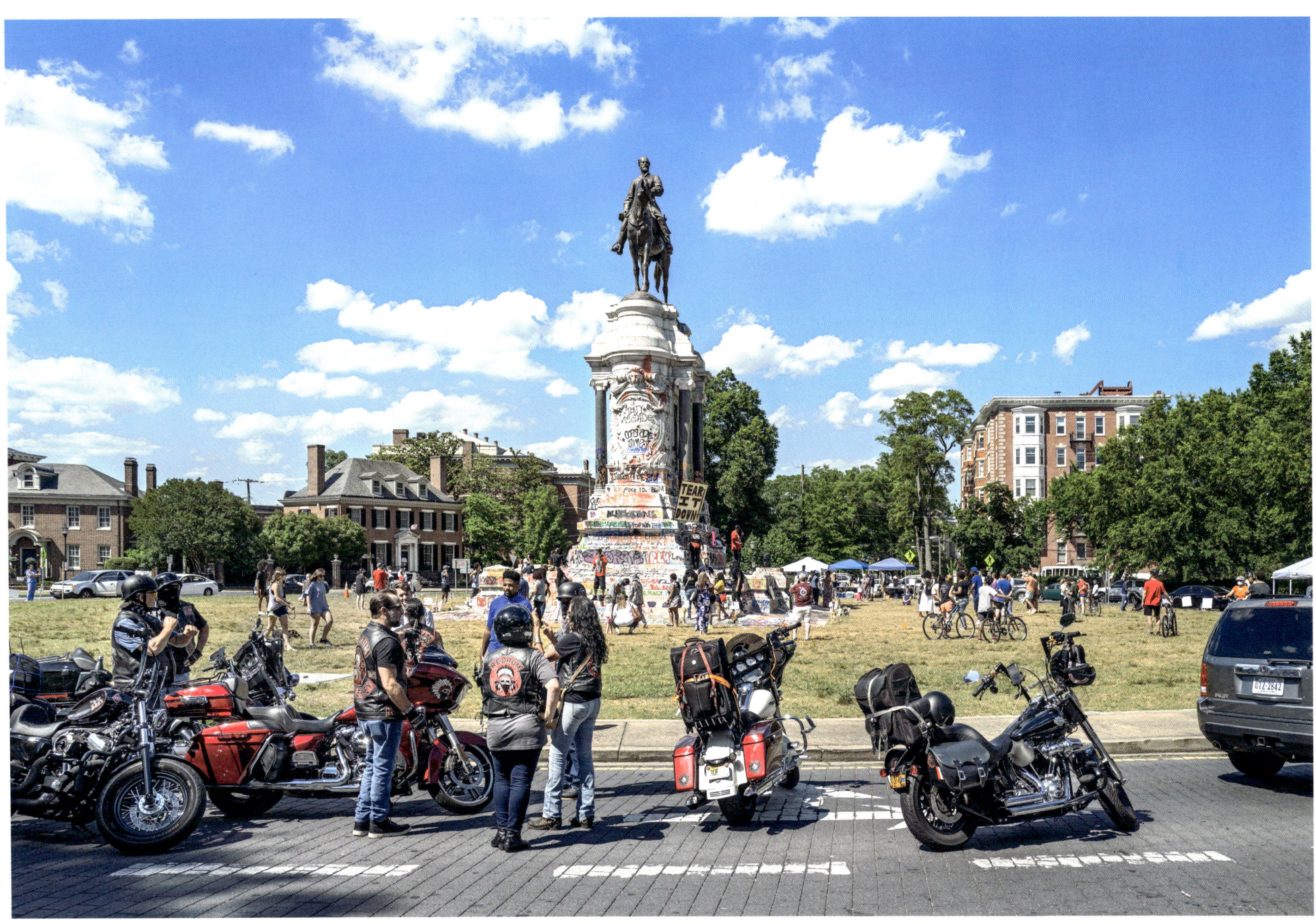

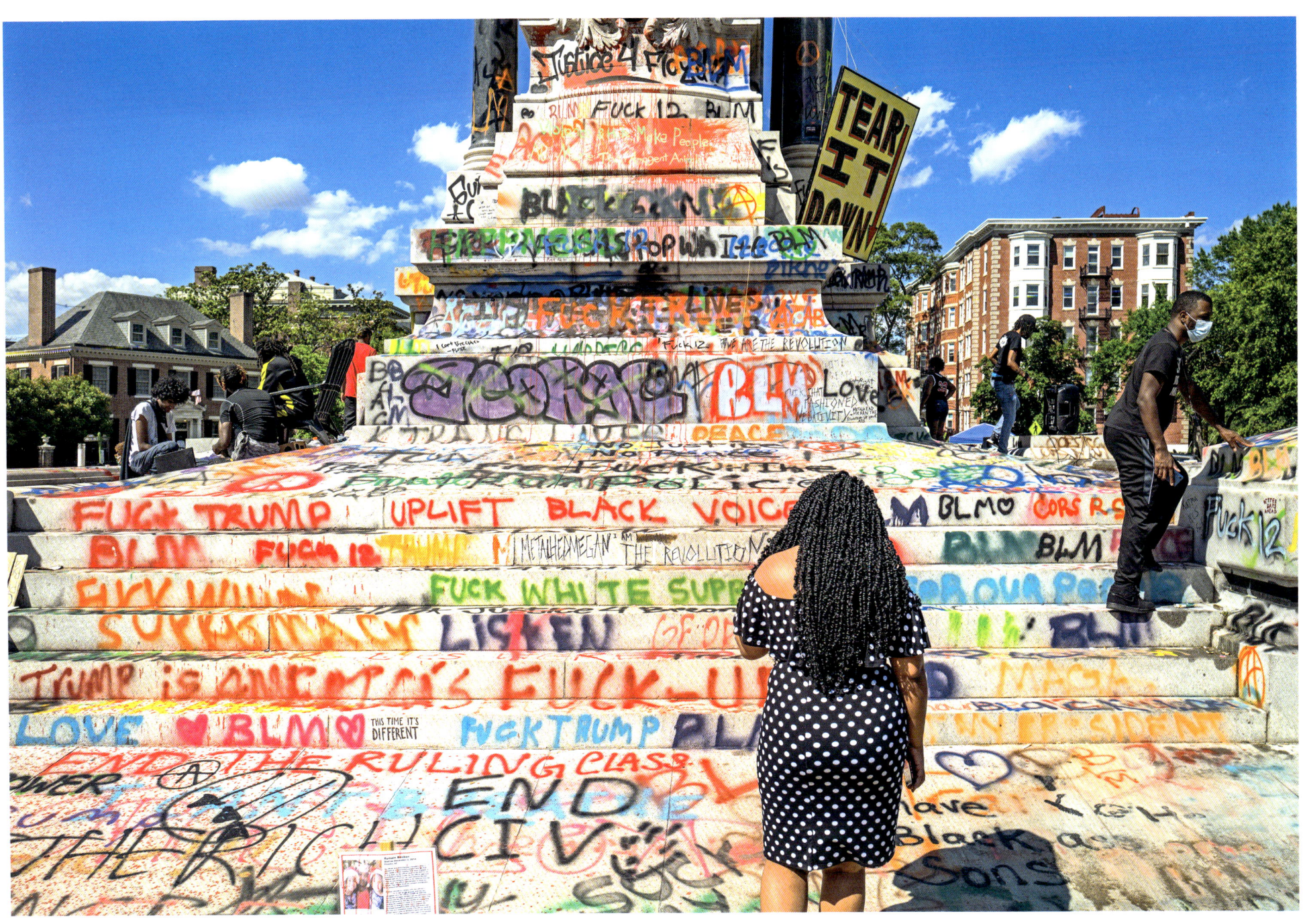

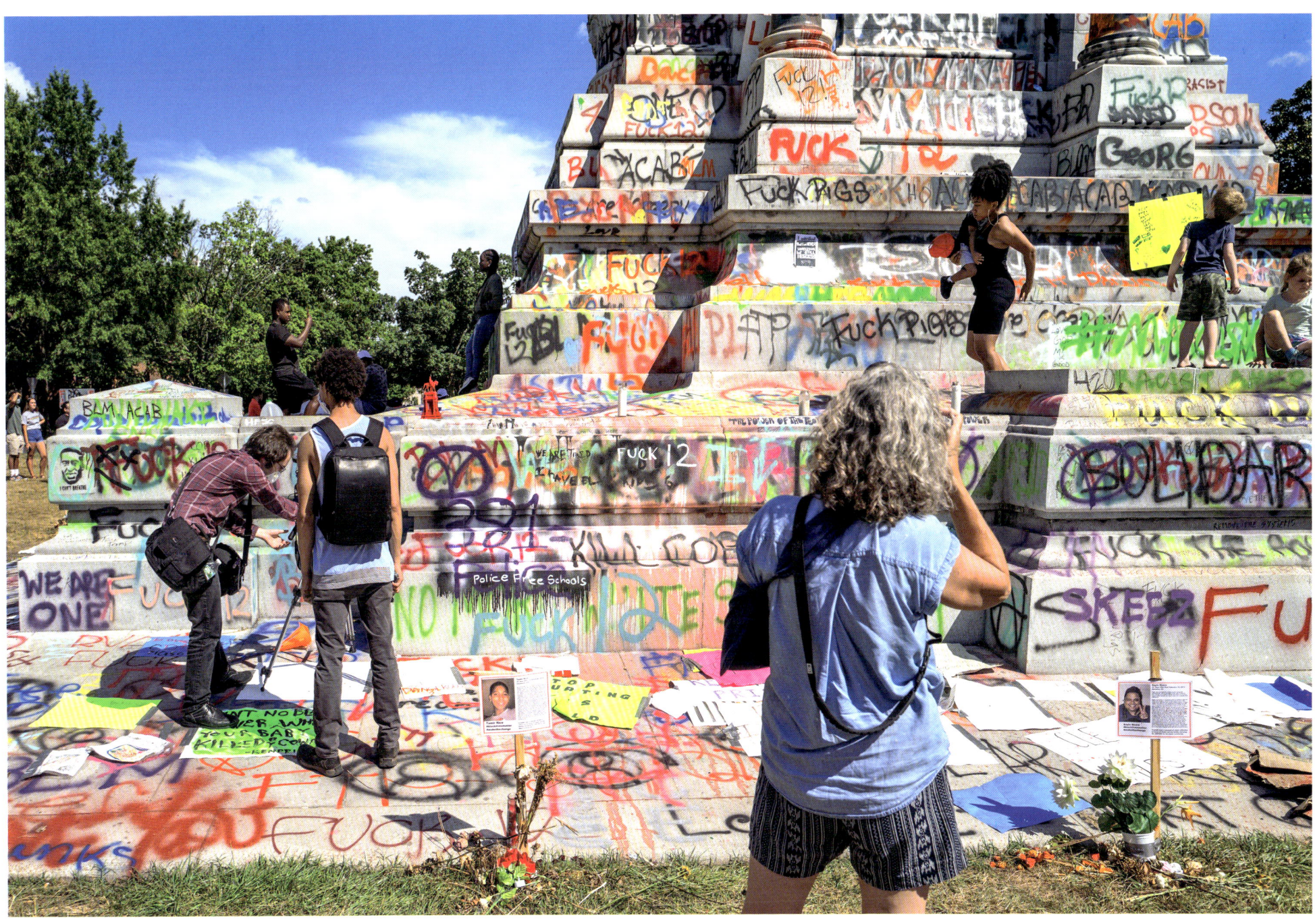

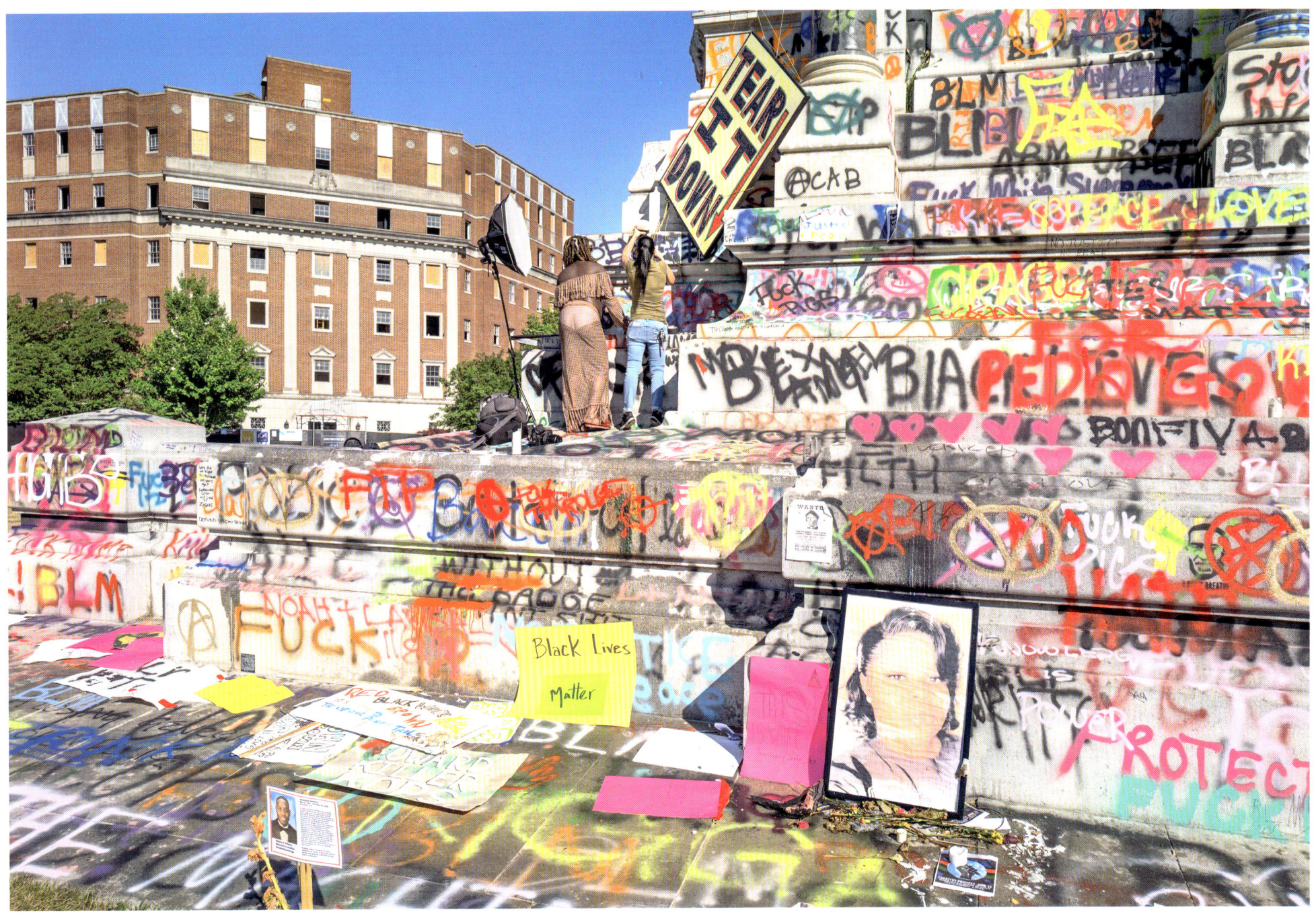

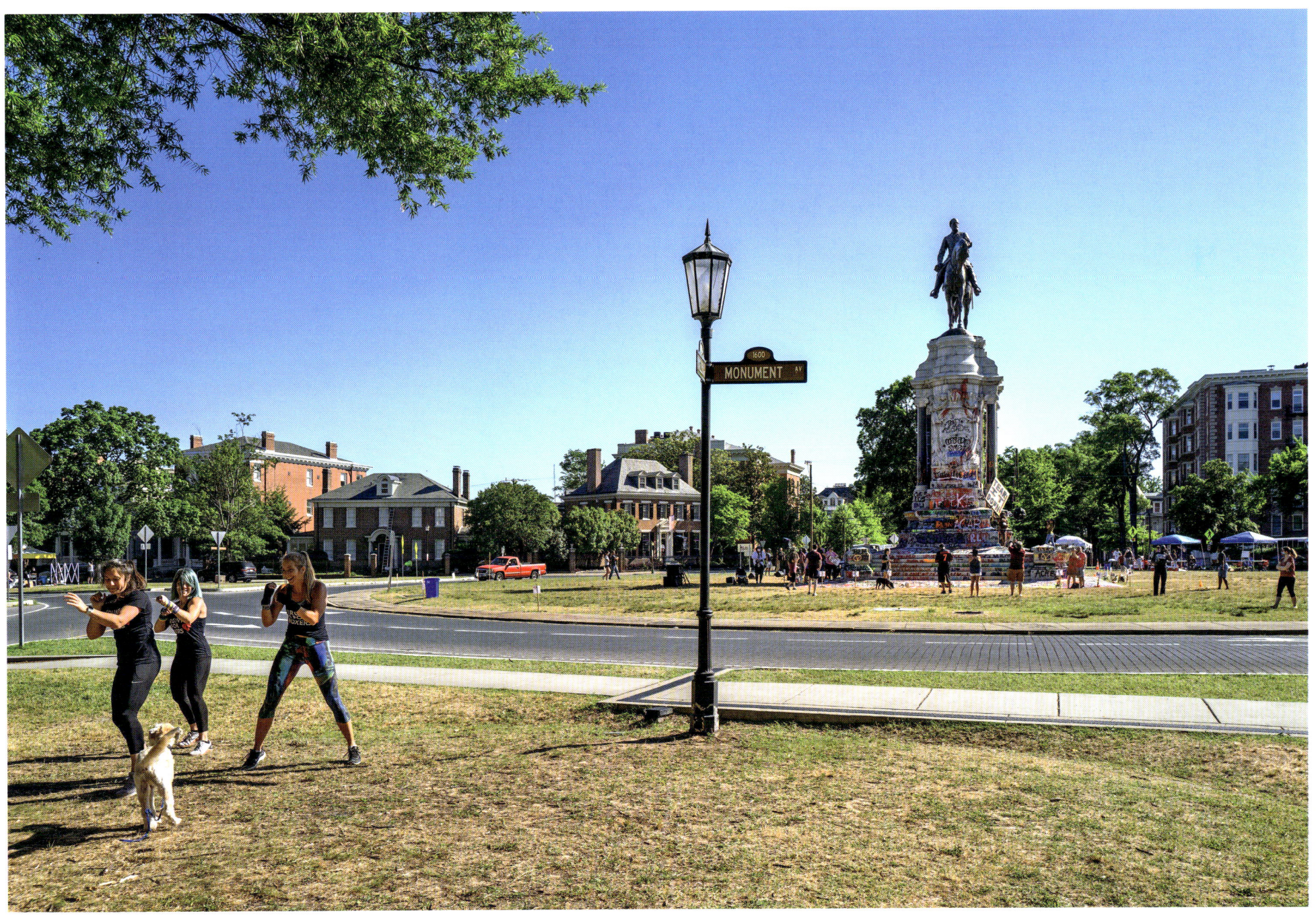

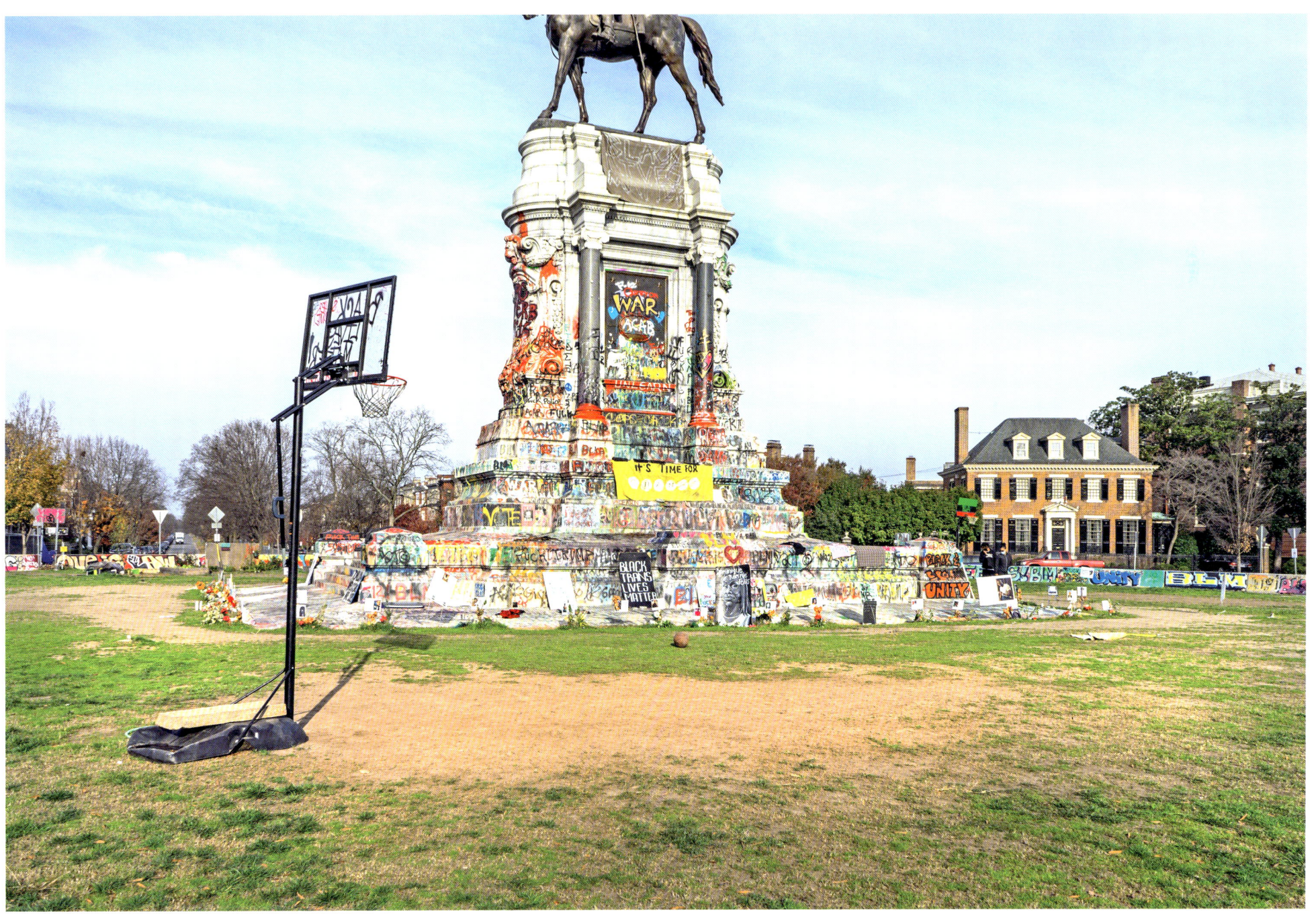

LEE DEFROCKED

The graffiti on the statue's base is now multilayered, words over images over more words. A palimpsest of messages has replaced the single narrative of greatness the statue once spoke, and an explosion of color has been overlaid on the old, pale blankness of the stone. Lee is no longer the focal point of the circle, but a ridiculous figure who seems to have wandered in on his horse from a cheesy Western or costume pageant. No one pays him any attention.

Philip Kennicott
The Washington Post
29 July 2020

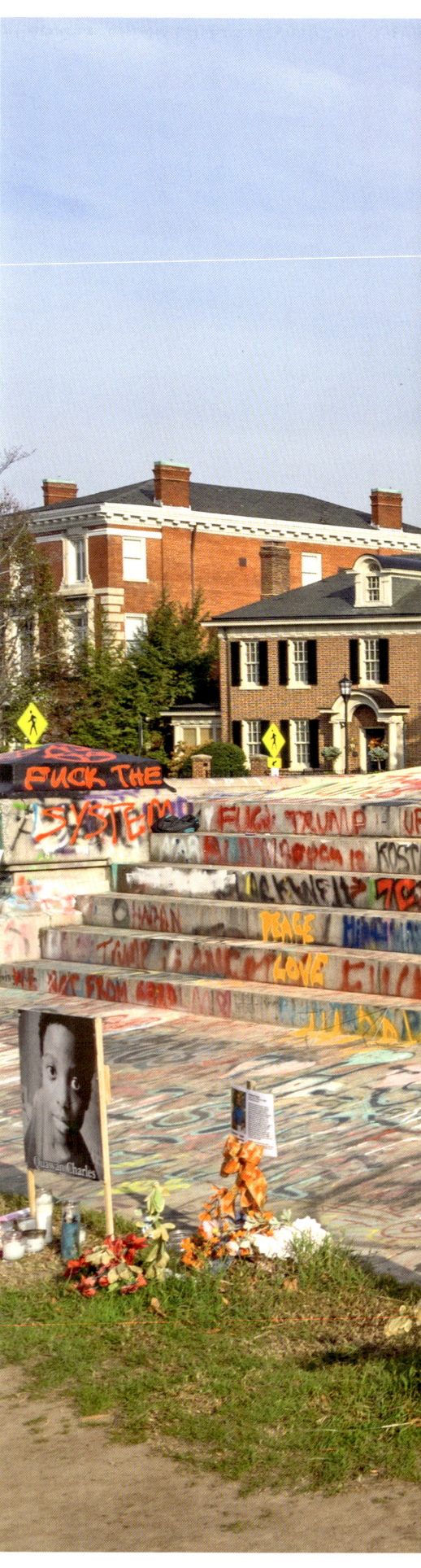

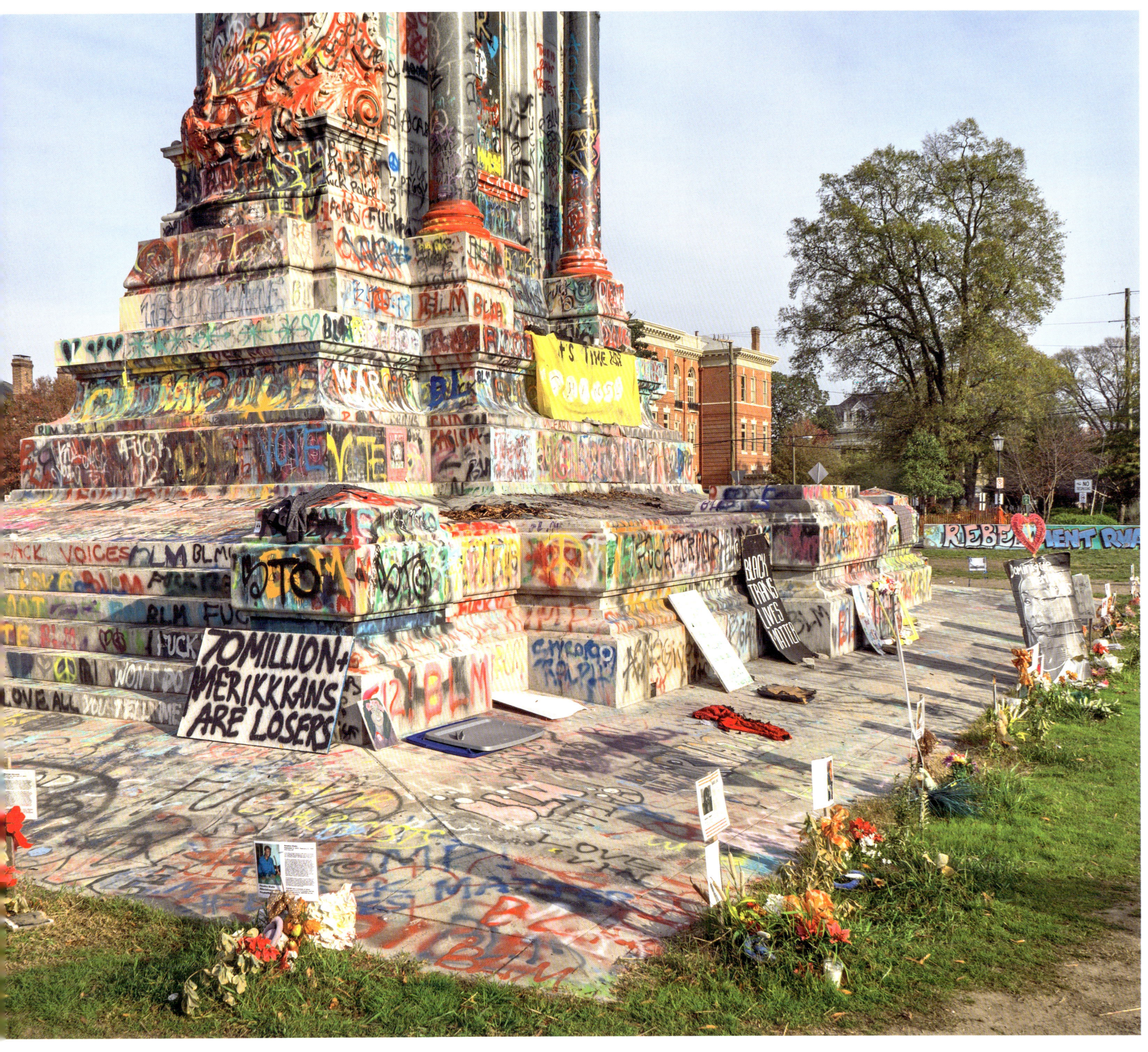

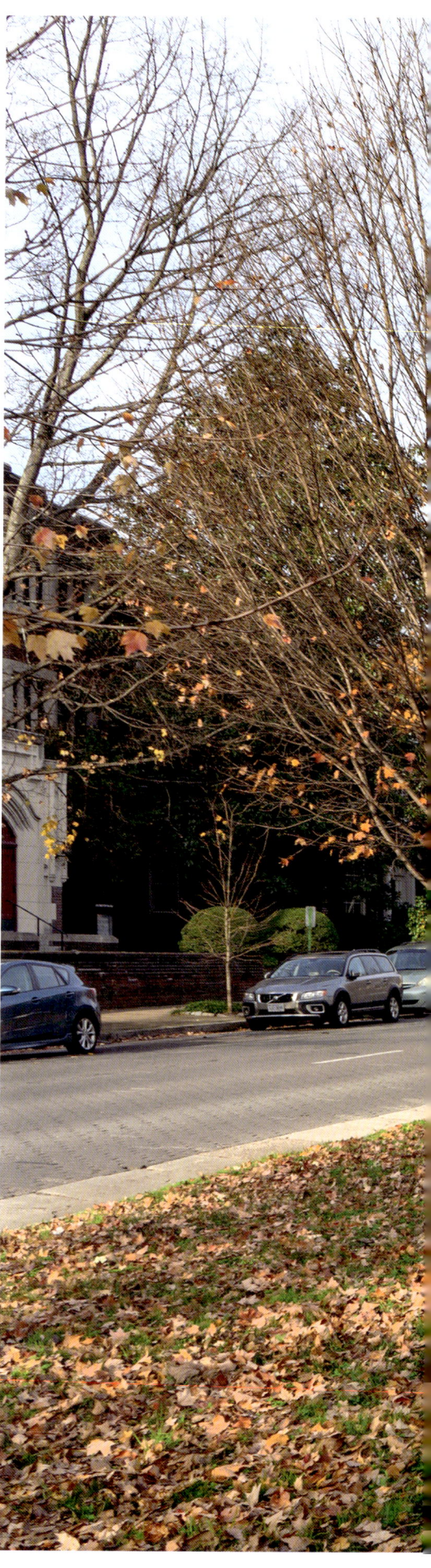

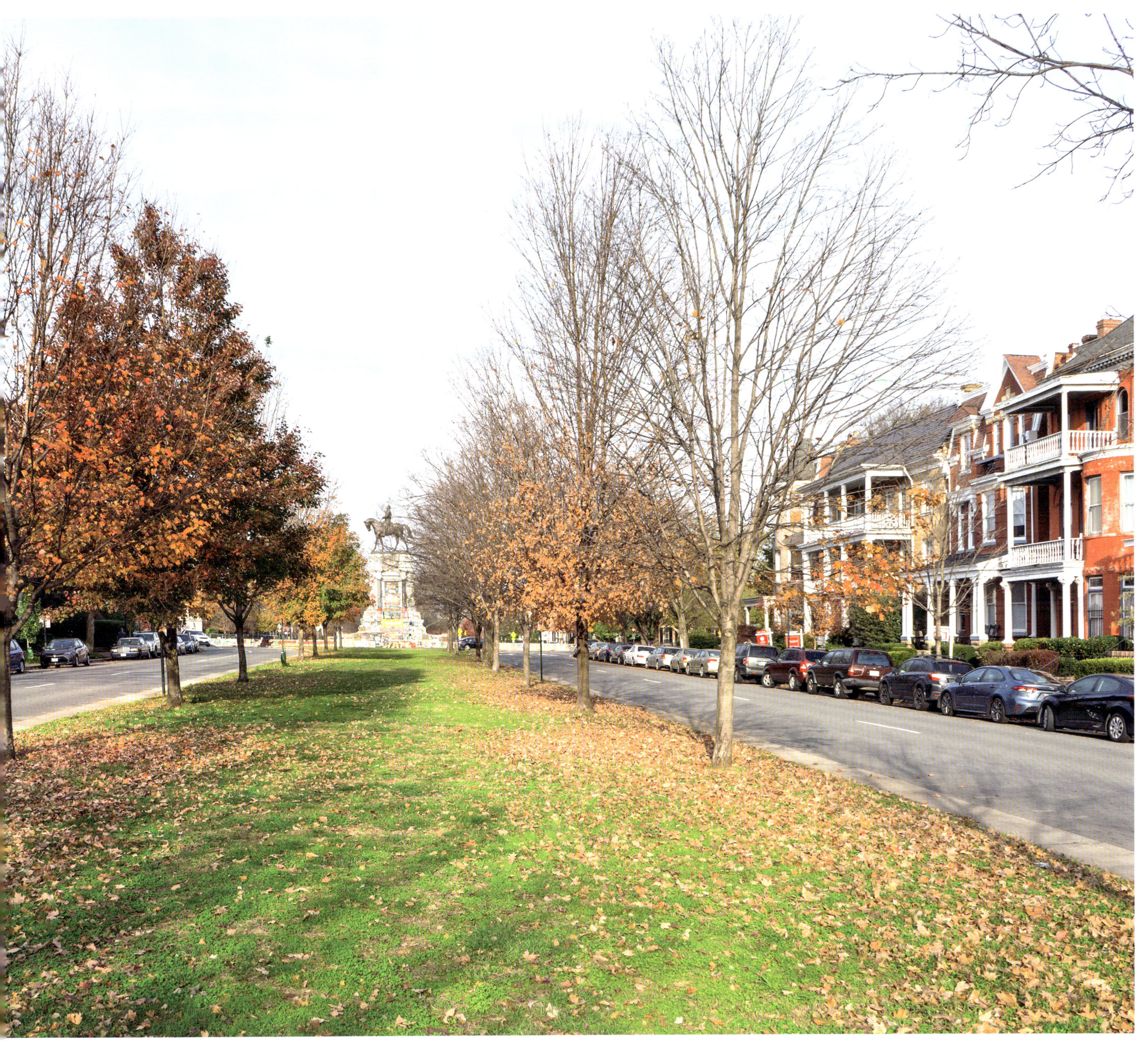

ROBERT E. LEE

It is the punishment of the South that its Robert Lees and Jefferson Davises will always be tall, handsome and well-born. That their courage will be physical and not moral. That their leadership will be weak compliance with public opinion and never costly and unswerving revolt for justice and right. It is ridiculous to seek to excuse Robert Lee as the most formidable agency this nation ever raised to make 4 million human beings goods instead of men. Either he knew what slavery meant when he helped maim and murder thousands in its defense, or he did not. If he did not he was a fool. If he did, Robert Lee was a traitor and a rebel – not indeed to his country, but to humanity and humanity's God.

W.E.B. Du Bois
1931

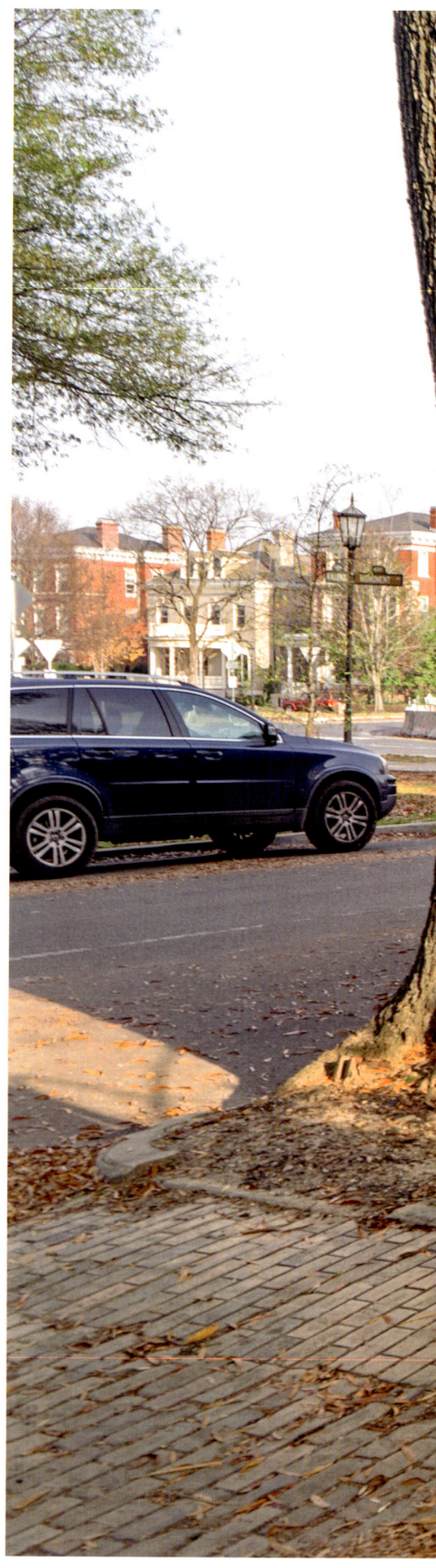

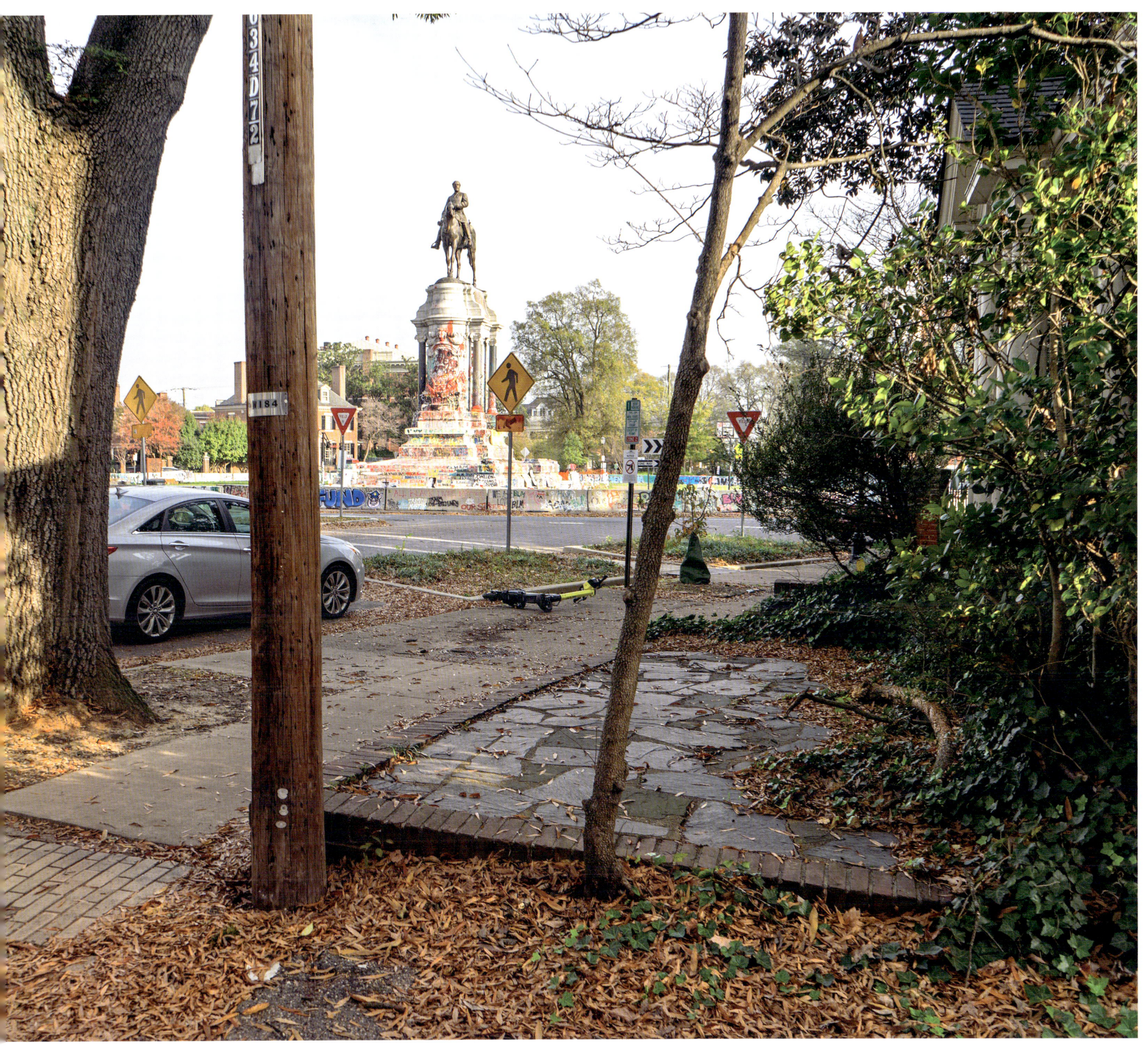

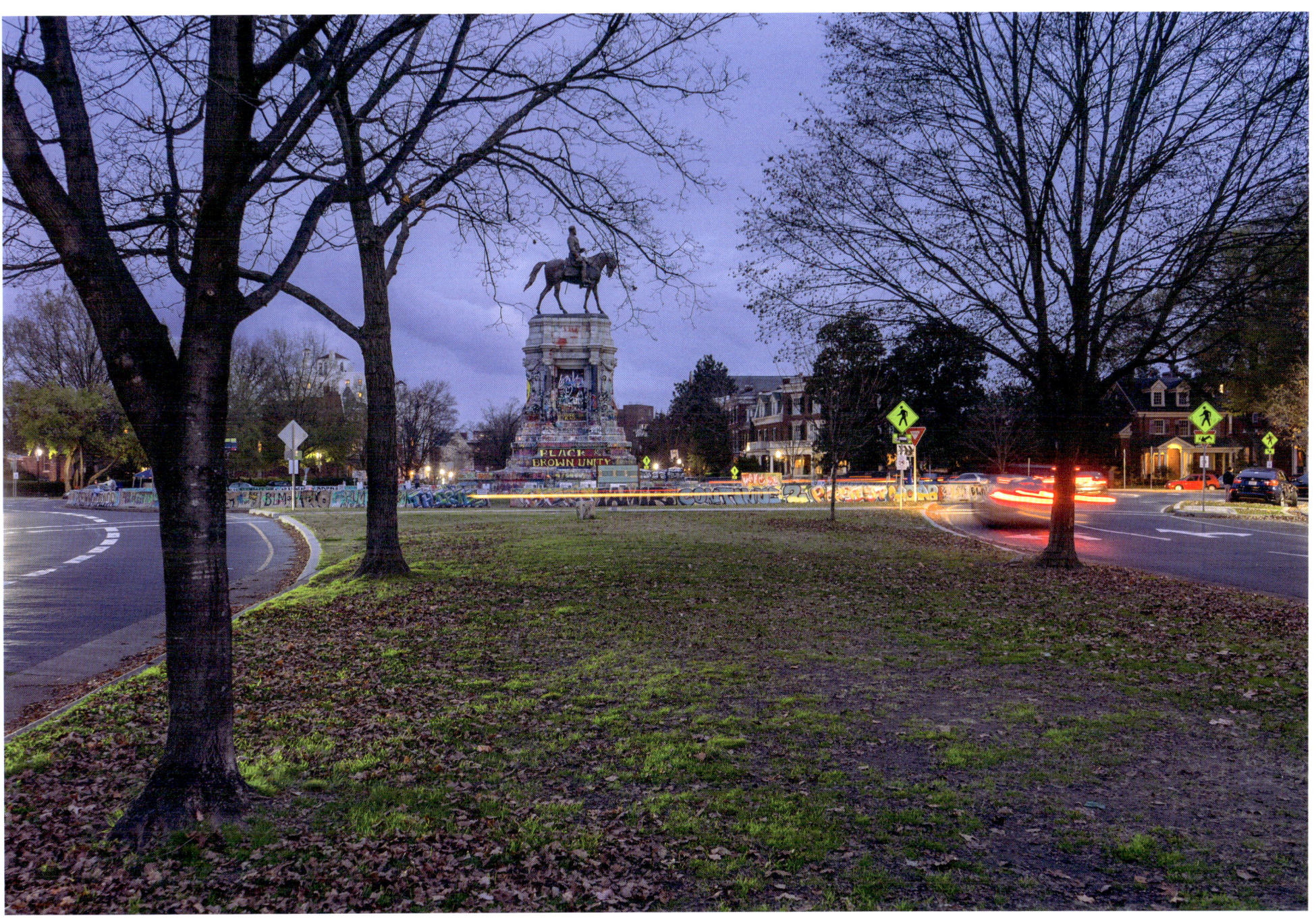

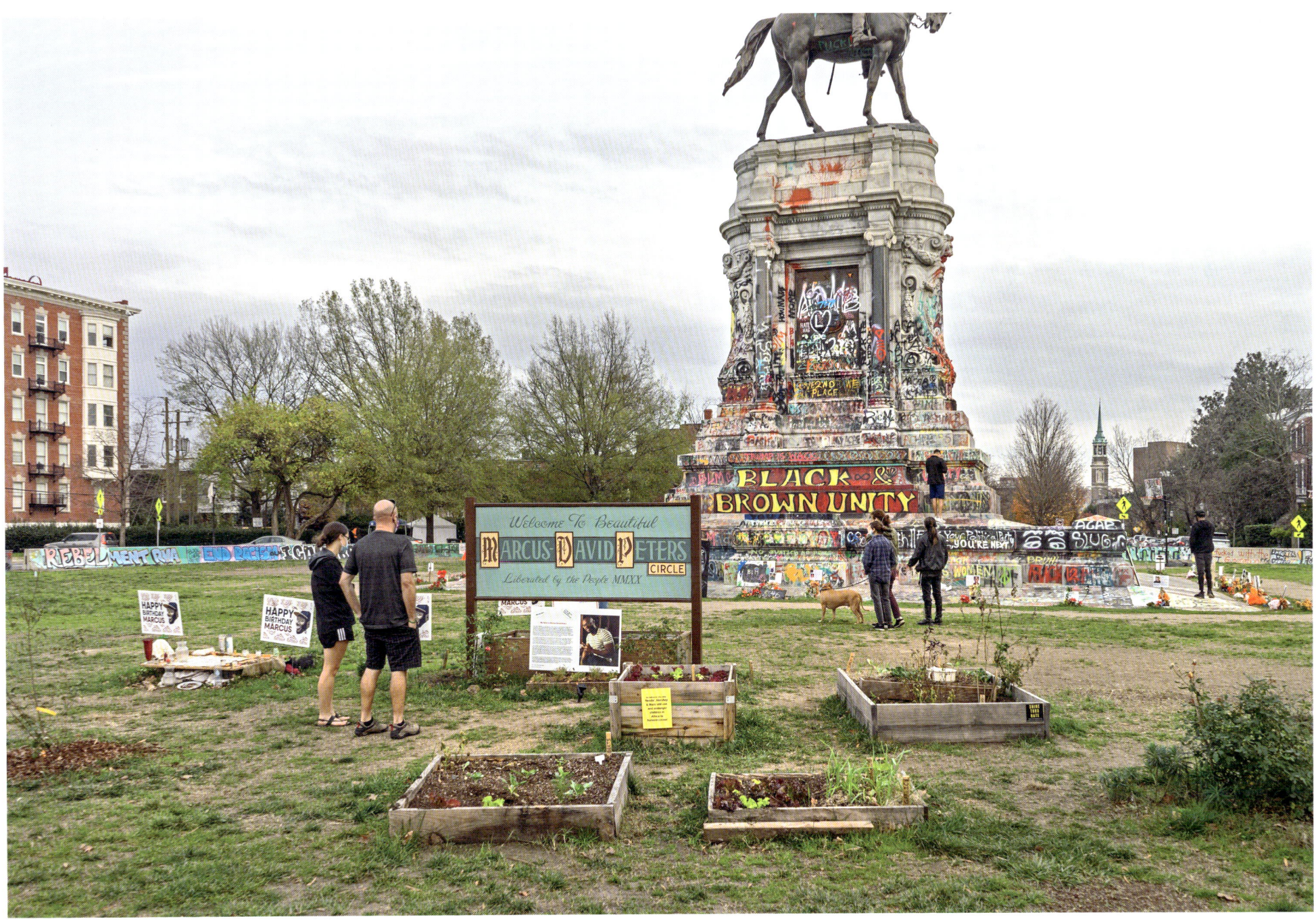

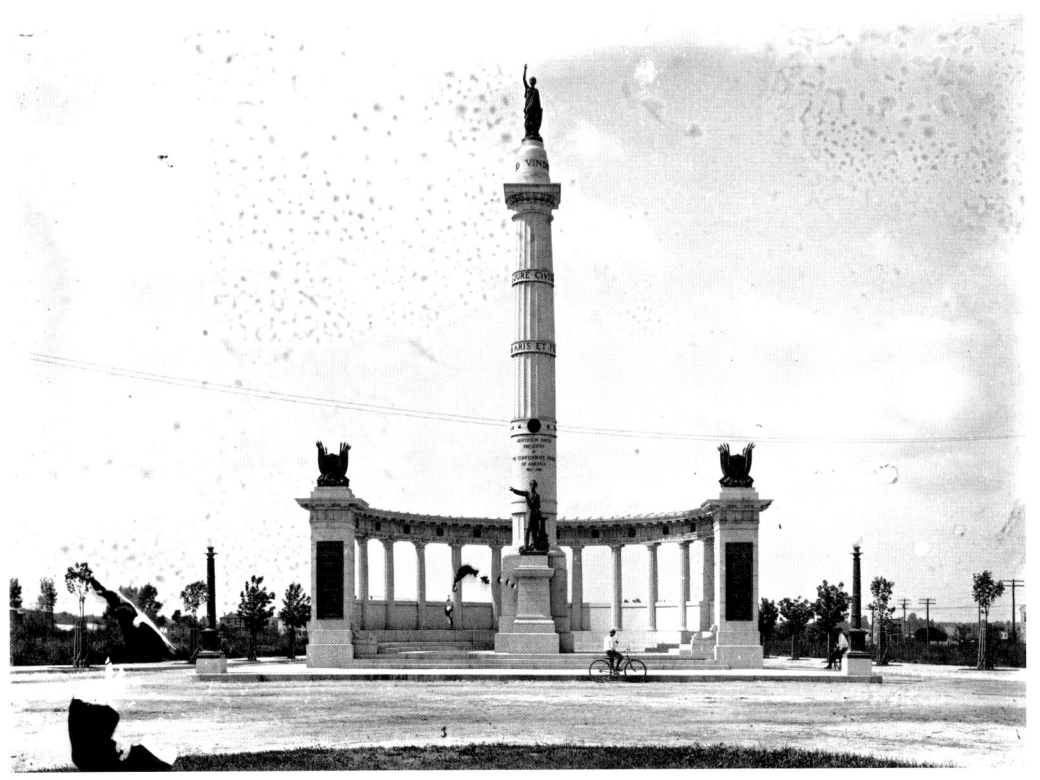

JEFFERSON DAVIS MEMORIAL, 1907

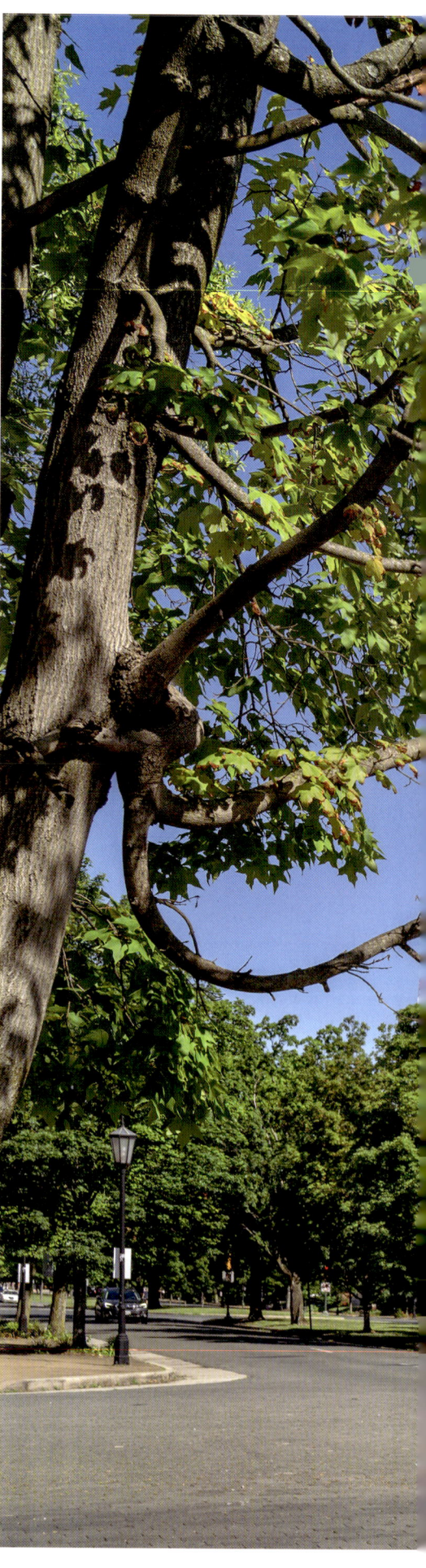

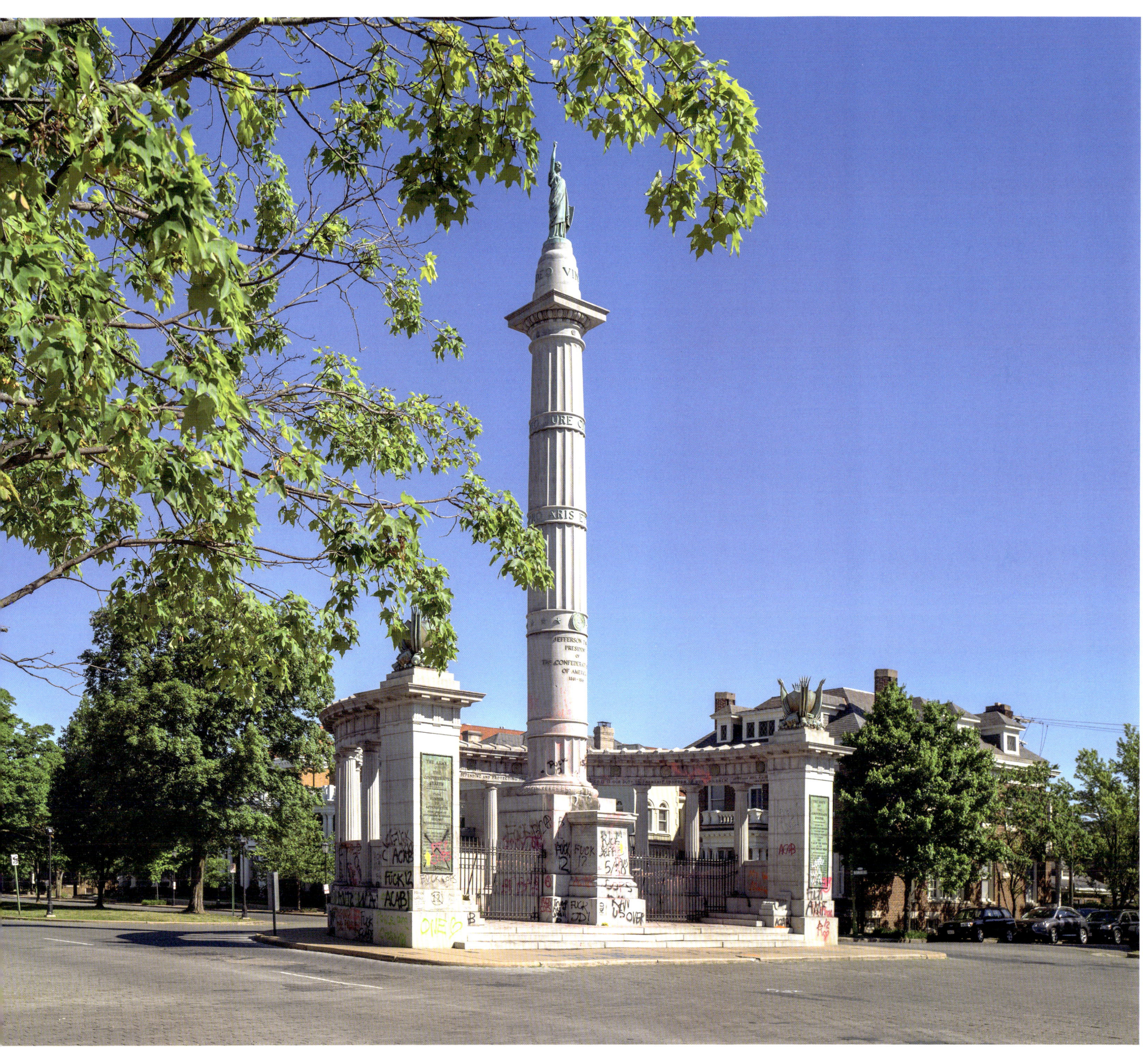

JEFFERSON DAVIS

Never before has there been seen such enthusiasm, never has there been displayed such a warm bond of blood and patriotism, never have those of a younger generation entered so closely into the spirit of the trying days of two-score years and more.

The occasion was a vindication of President Davis, an utter rout for the army of slanderers, and above all a noble tribute to the memory of the 'Lost Cause'.

The Times Dispatch
4 June 1907

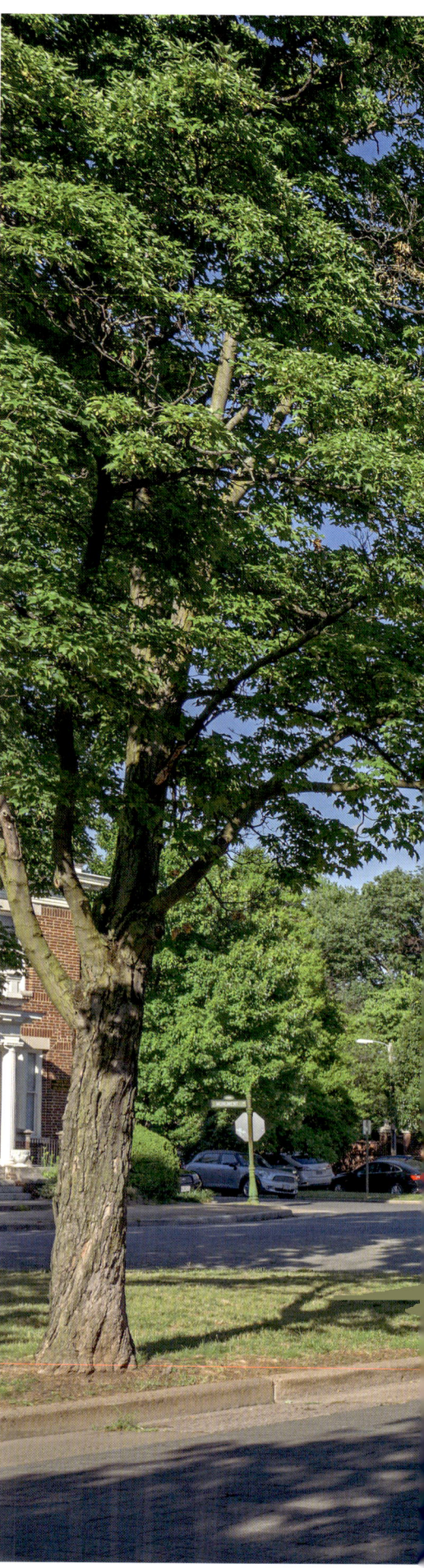

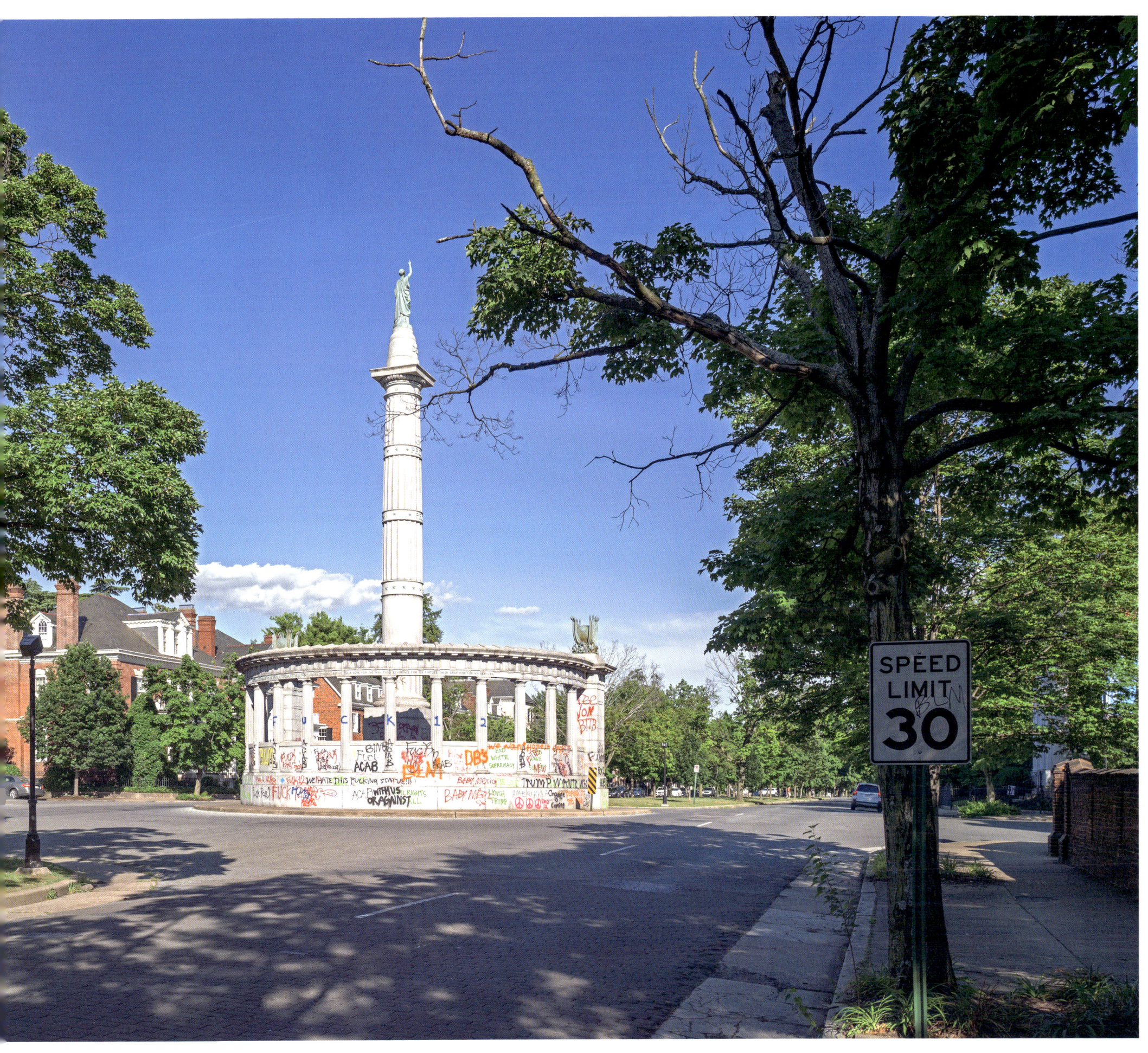

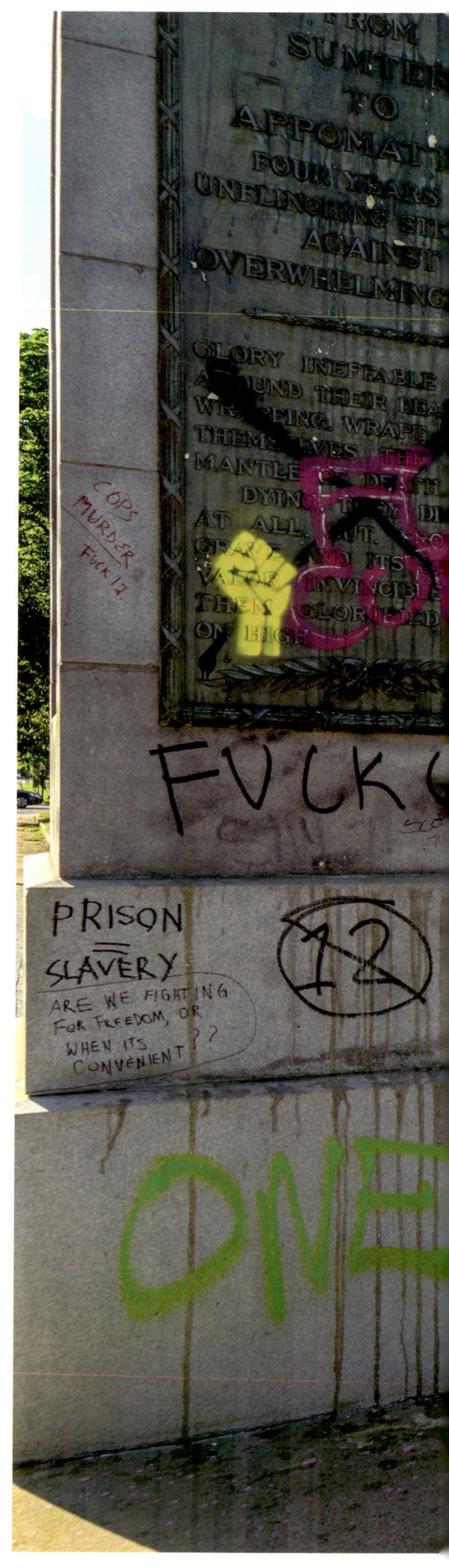

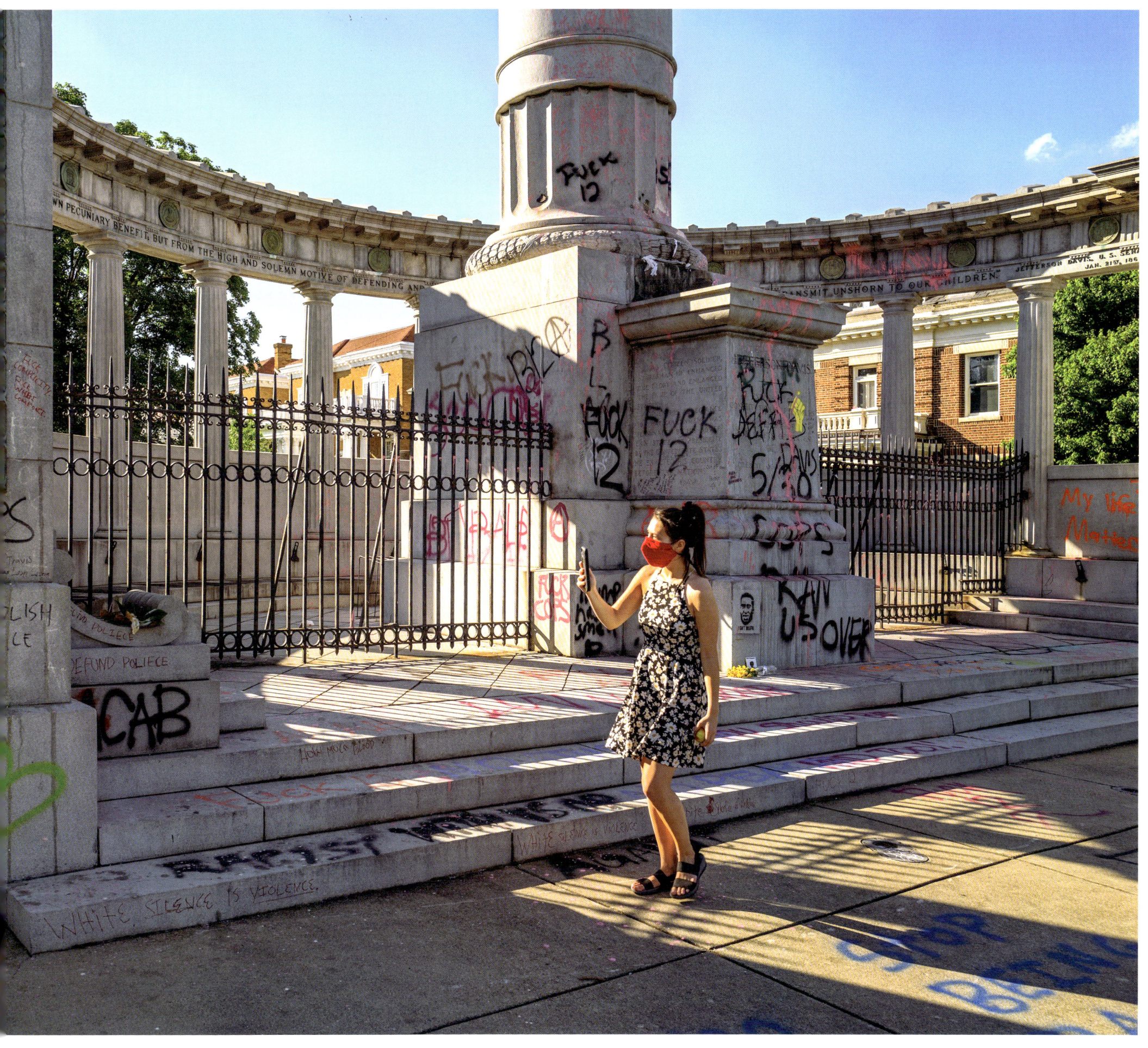

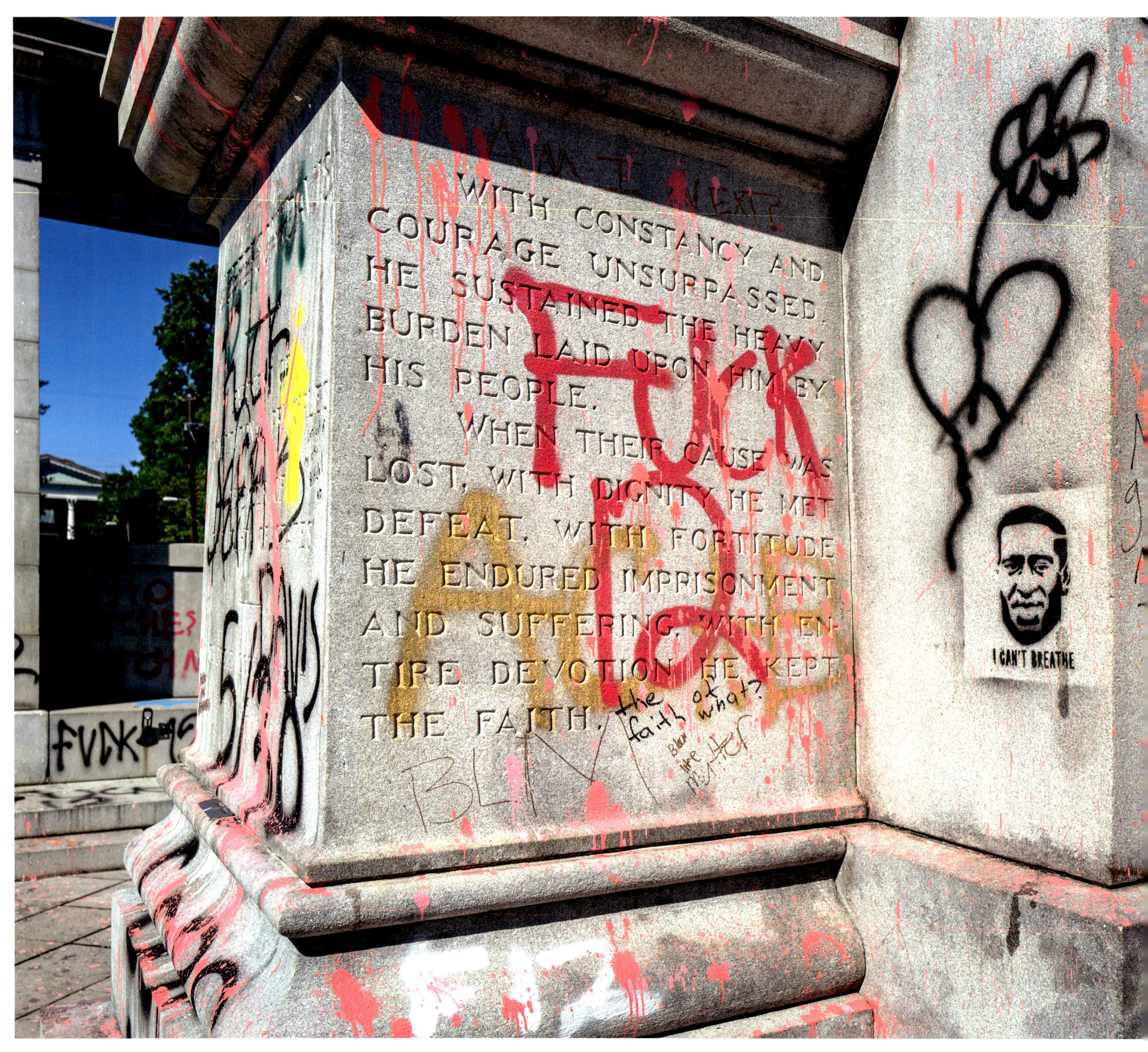

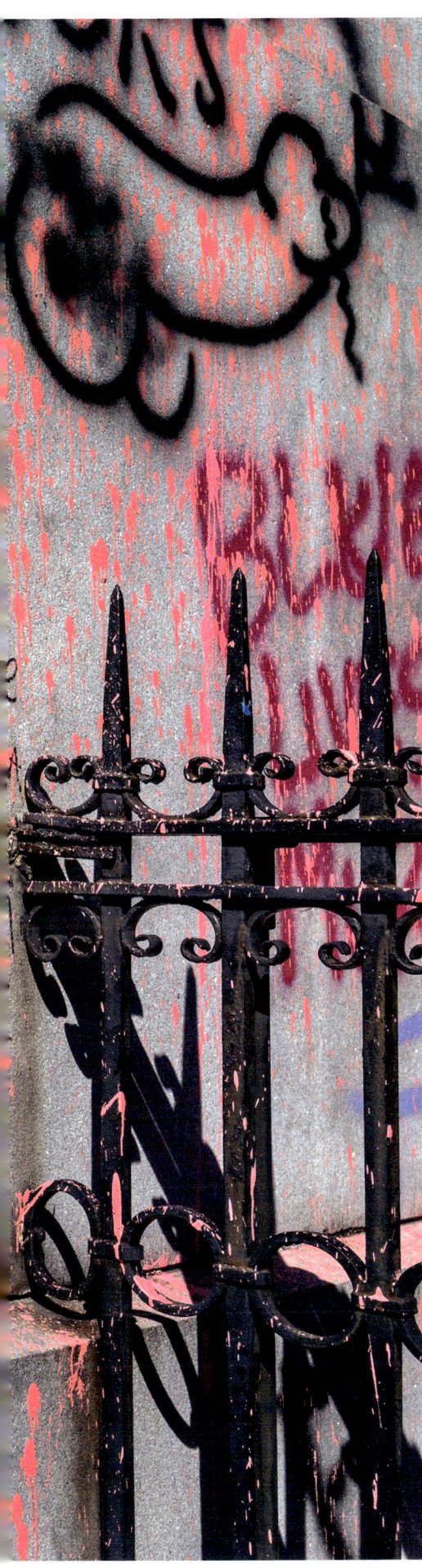

ANOTHER VIRGINIA LYNCHING

The lynching of JOHN HENRY JAMES, (colored) was as dastardly in its conception and as heinous in its execution as the crime with which he stood charged.

On the afternoon of July 11th, about four miles from Charlottesville, Va., he was taken from the officers of the law and hanged to a tree.

The story of the brutal murder is revolting. We believe that the authorities were blamable. They know that it was risky to bring this man unprotected to Charlottesville.

JAMES died protesting his innocence to the last. We do not believe that any effort will be made to punish the murderers. They boldly perpetrated their crime and virtually defied the commonwealth.

There was no effort made to conceal their identity. The guilt or the innocence of James does not enter into the question.

The Richmond Planet
July 16 1898

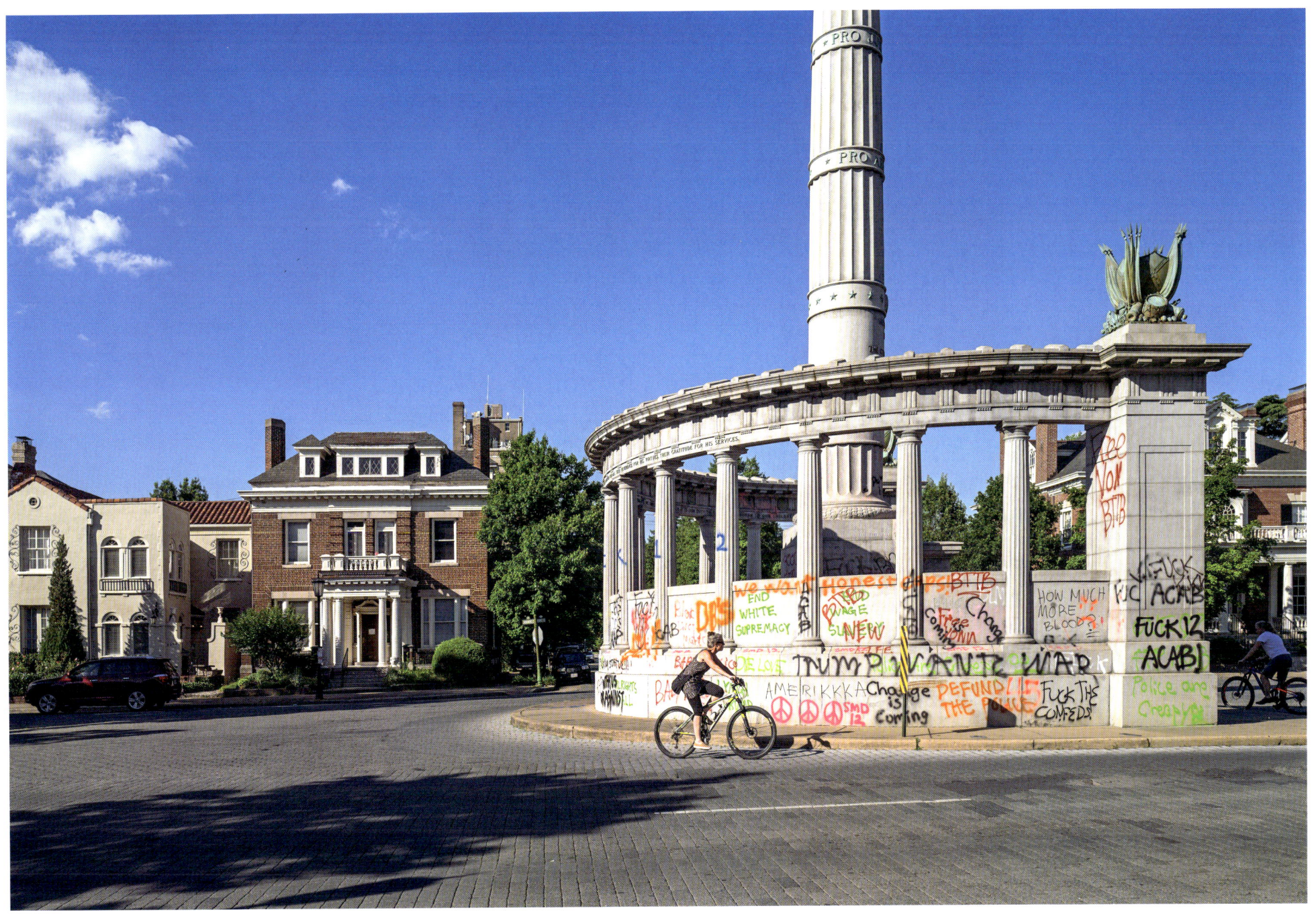

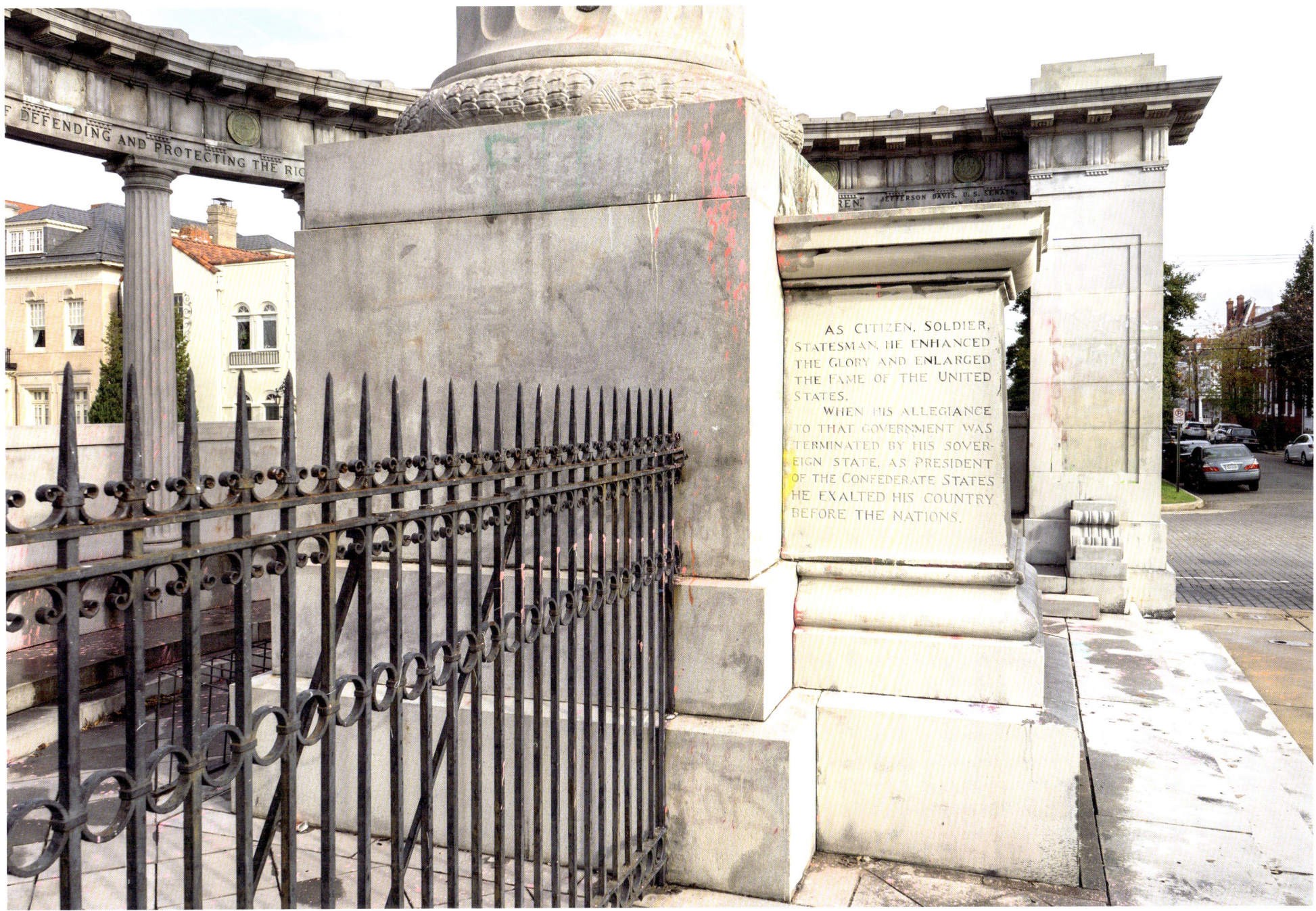

F DEFENDING AND PROTECTING THE RIG

AS CITIZEN, SOLDIER,
STATESMAN, HE ENHANCED
THE GLORY AND ENLARGED
THE FAME OF THE UNITED
STATES.
WHEN HIS ALLEGIANCE
TO THAT GOVERNMENT WAS
TERMINATED BY HIS SOVER-
EIGN STATE, AS PRESIDENT
OF THE CONFEDERATE STATES
HE EXALTED HIS COUNTRY
BEFORE THE NATIONS.

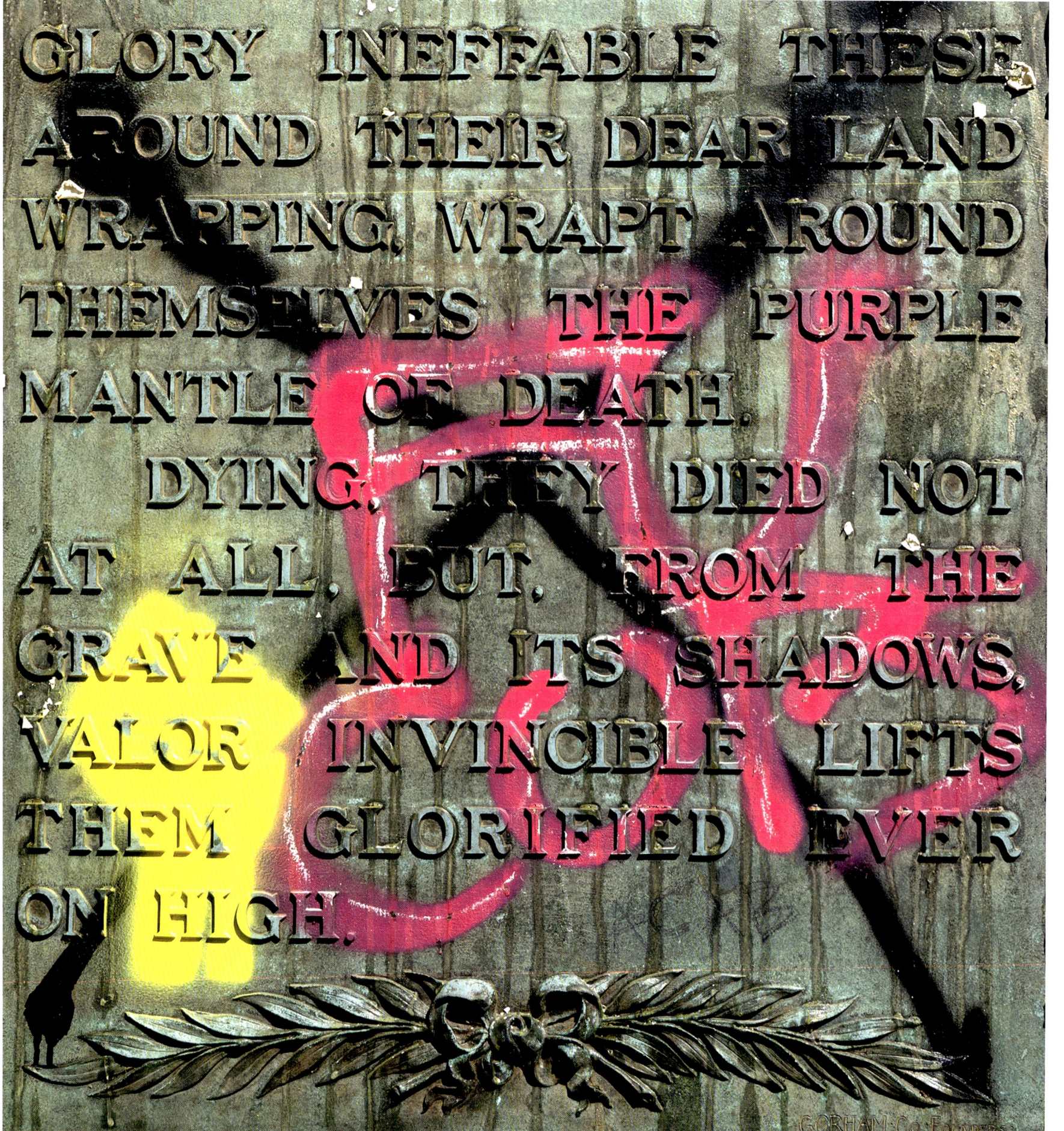

IF TO DIE NOBLY BE EVER
THE PROUDEST GLORY OF
VIRTUE, THIS OF ALL MEN
HAS FORTUNE GREATLY
GRANTED TO THEM, FOR,
YEARNING WITH DEEP
DESIRE TO CLOTHE THEIR
COUNTRY WITH FREEDOM
NOW AT THE LAST
THEY REST FULL OF
AN AGELESS FAME

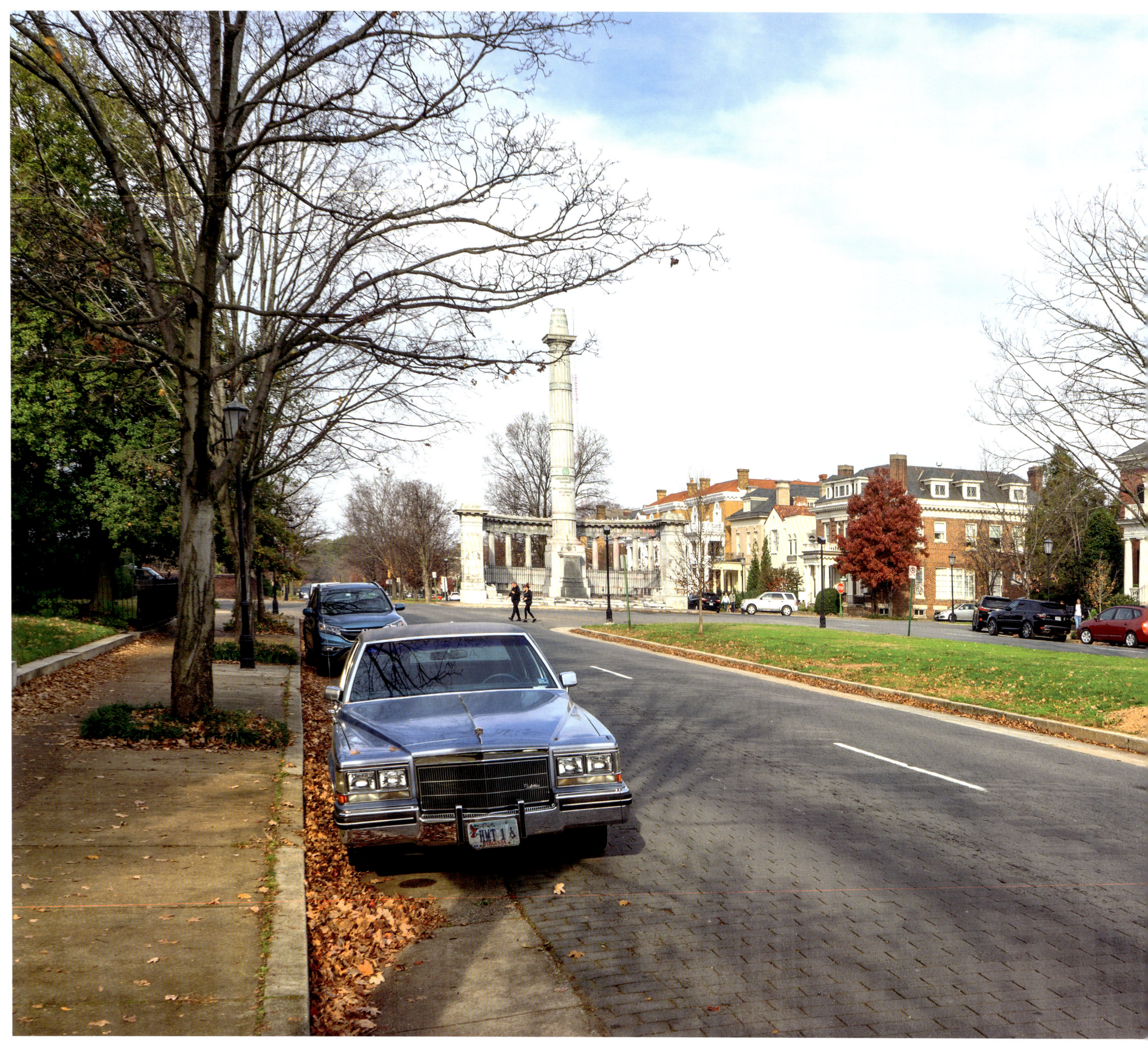

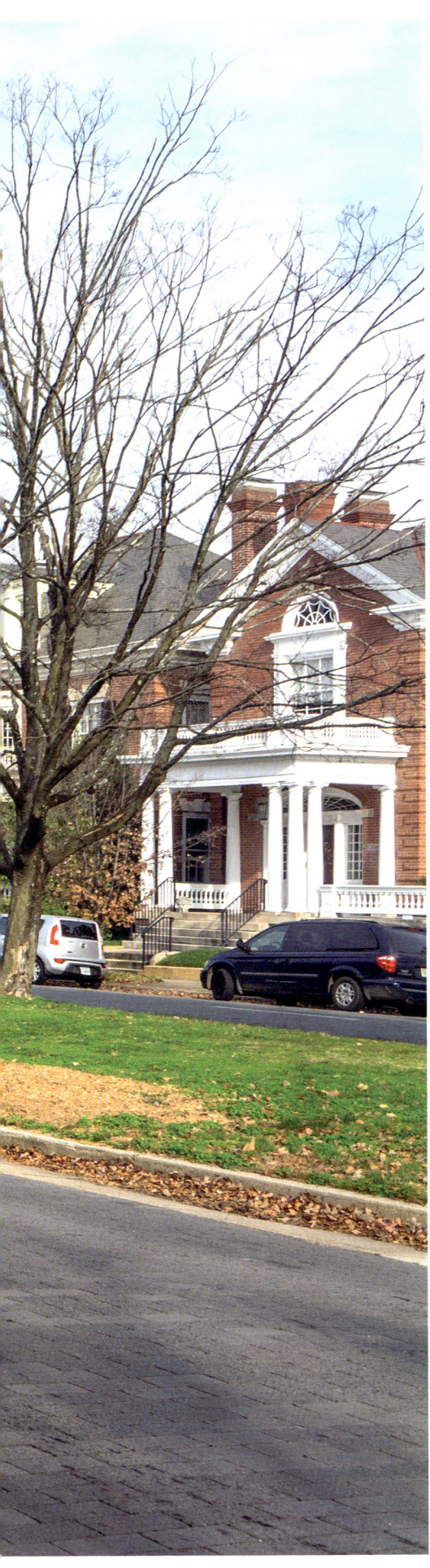

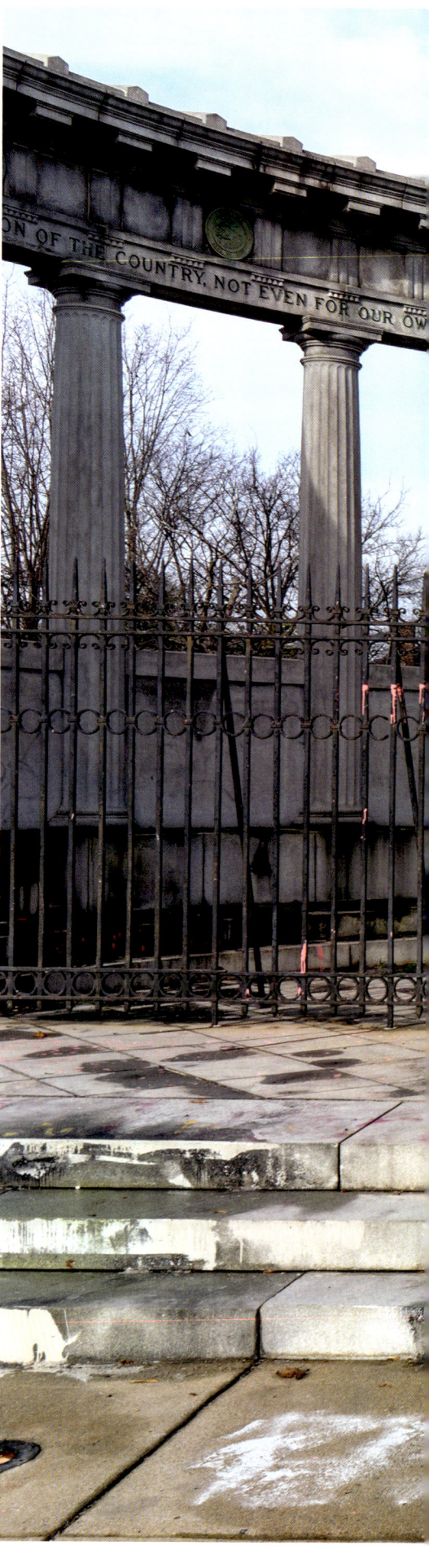

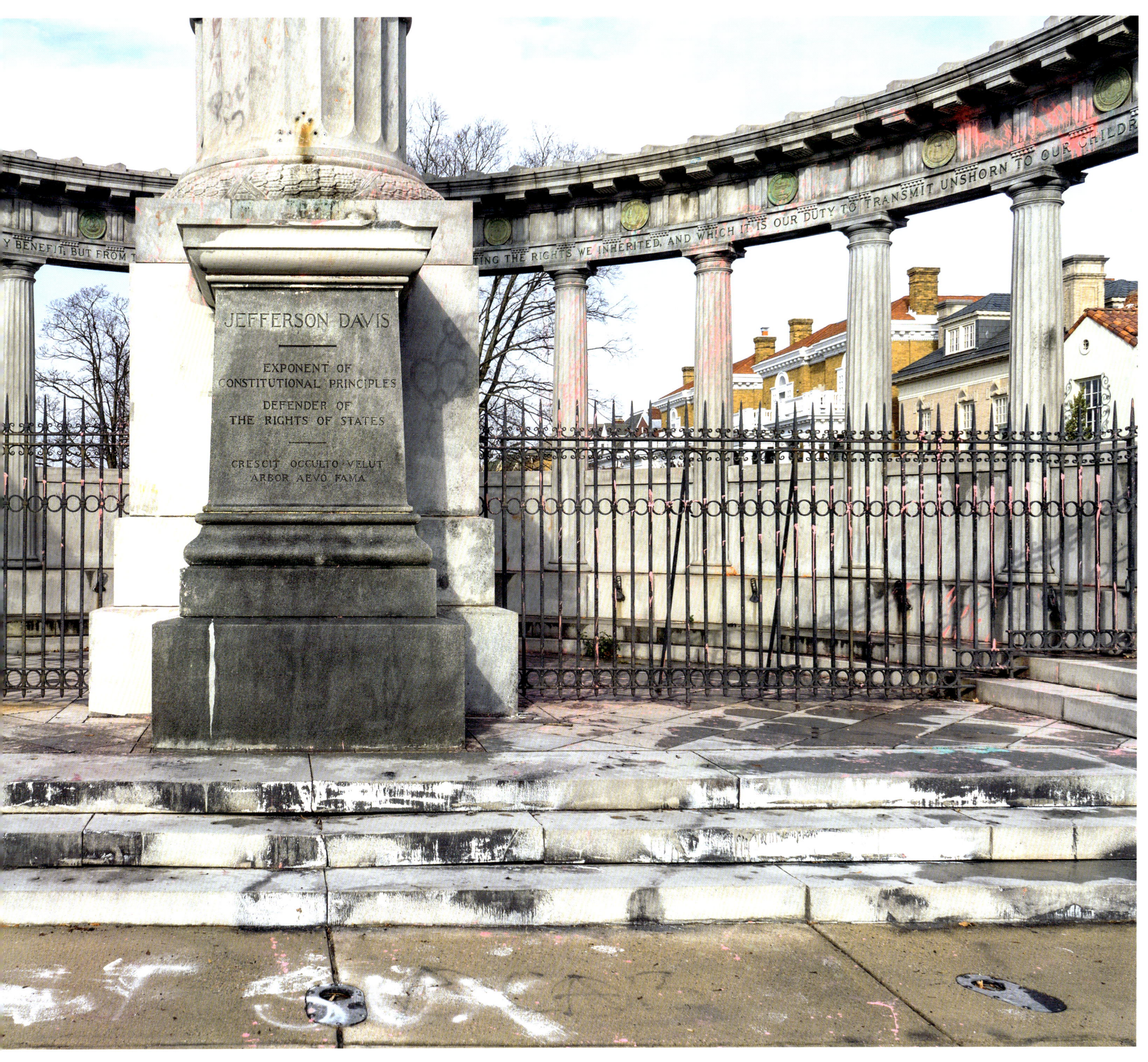

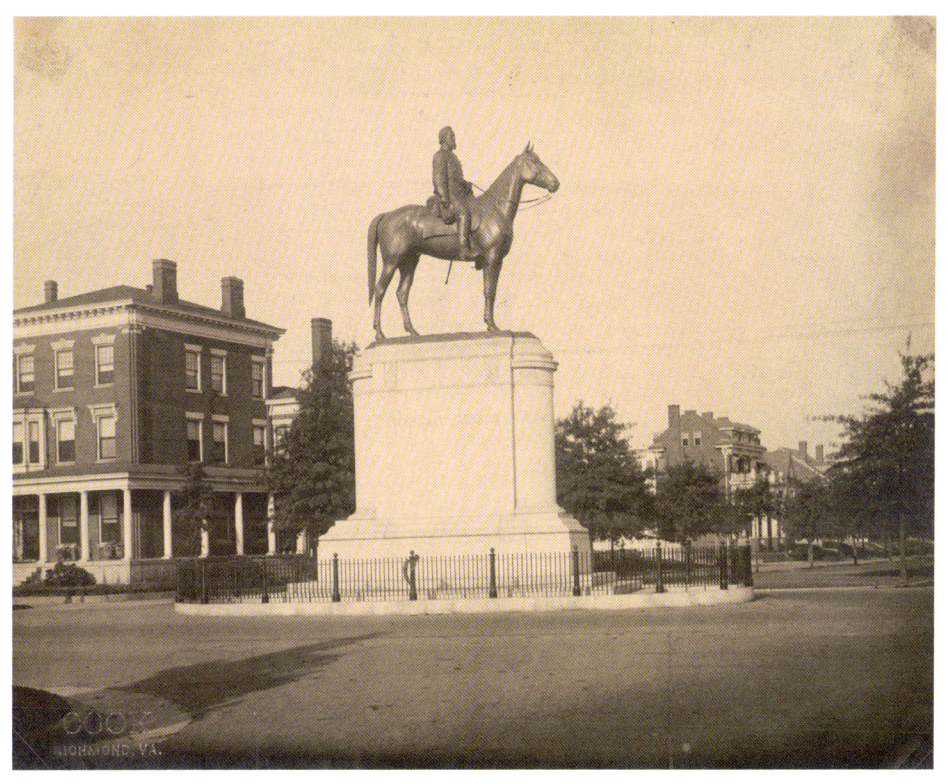

STONEWALL JACKSON MONUMENT, 1919

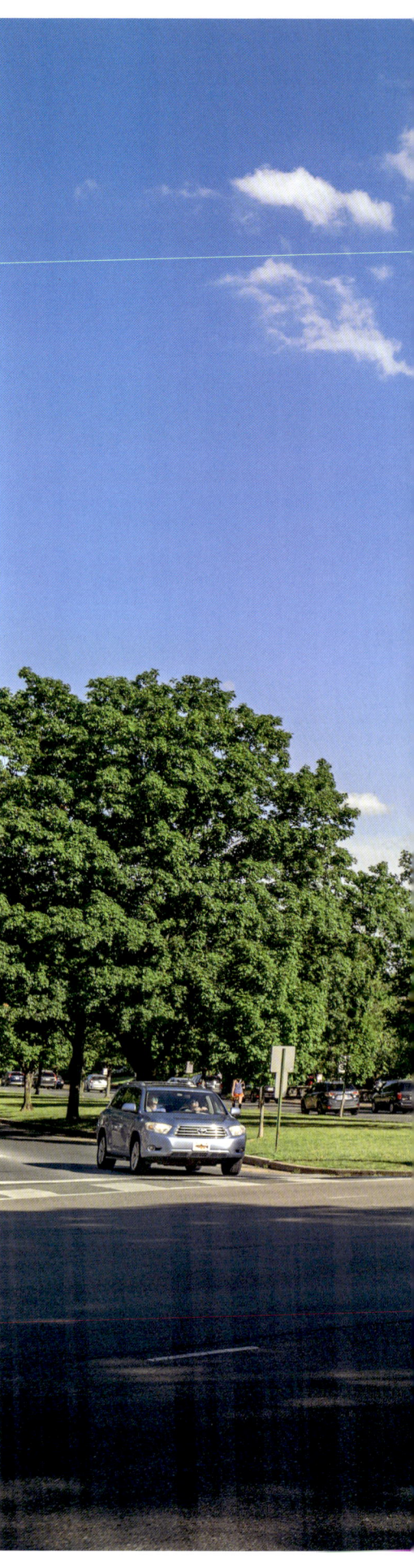

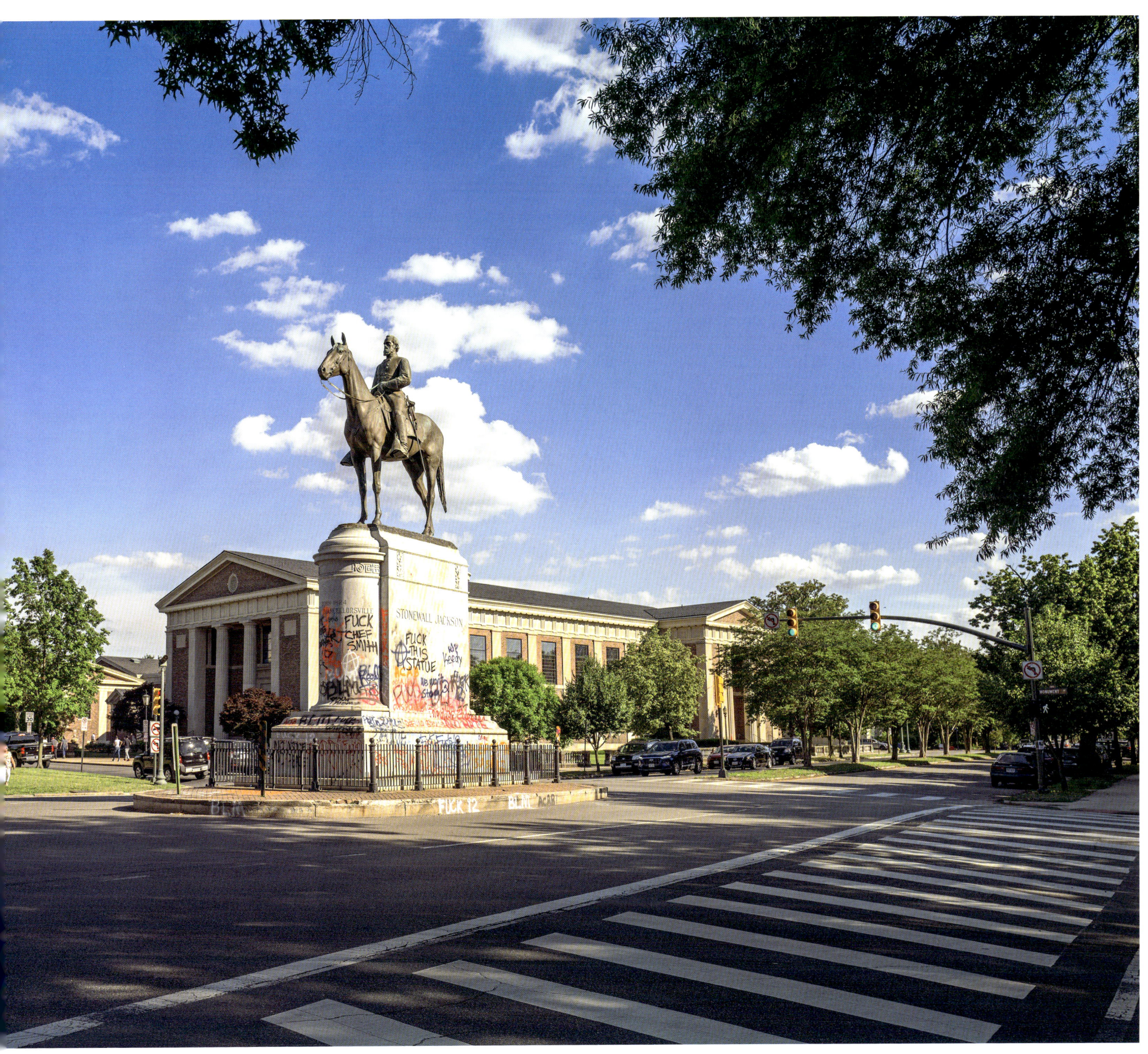

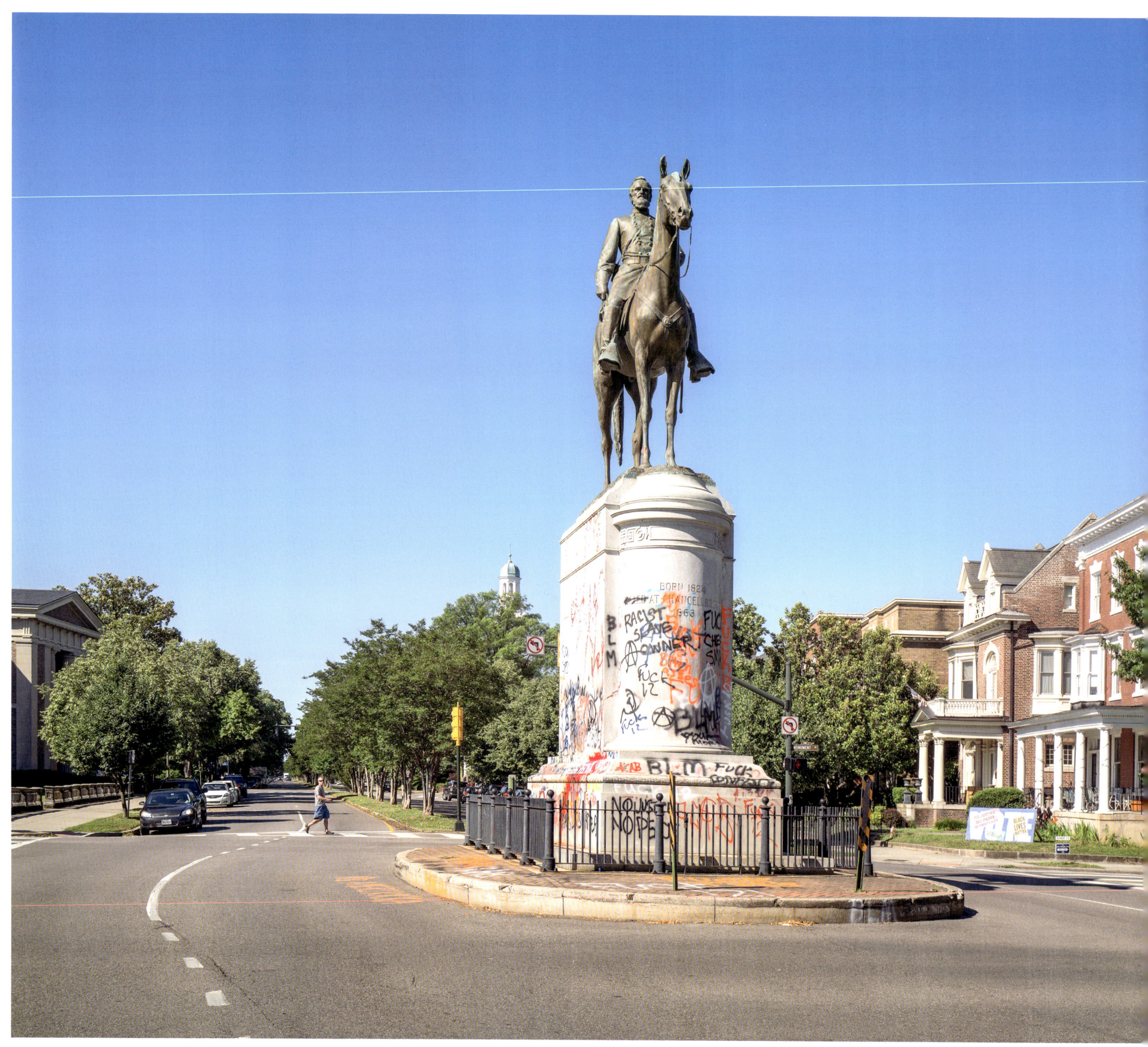

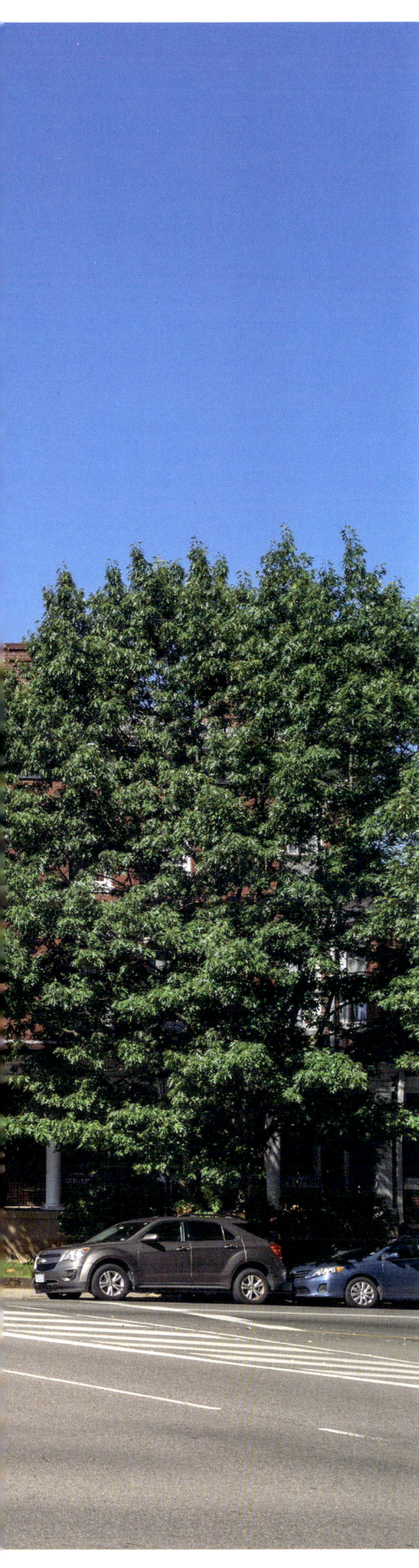

STONEWALL JACKSON

Dear Richmond Mayor Levar Stoney and members of the Monument Avenue Commission,

While we do not purport to speak for all of Stonewall's kin, our sense of justice leads us to believe that removing the Stonewall statue and other monuments should be part of a larger project of actively mending the racial disparities that hundreds of years of white supremacy have wrought. We hope other descendants of Confederate generals will stand with us.

As cities all over the South are realizing now, we are not in need of added context. We are in need of a new context – one in which the statues have been taken down.

Respectfully,

William Jackson Christian
Warren Edmund Christian
Great-great-grandsons
of Thomas Jonathan 'Stonewall' Jackson
16 August 2017

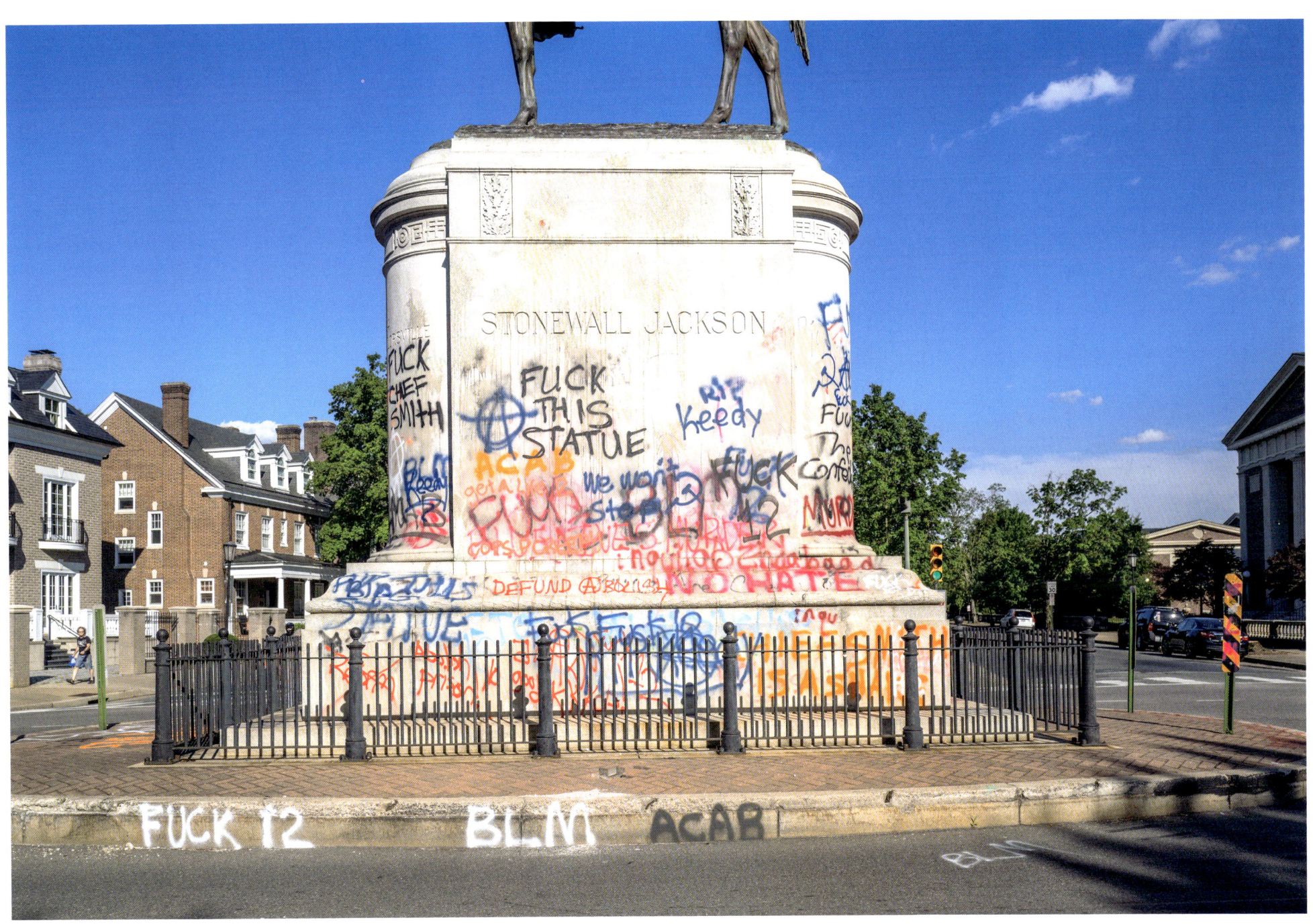

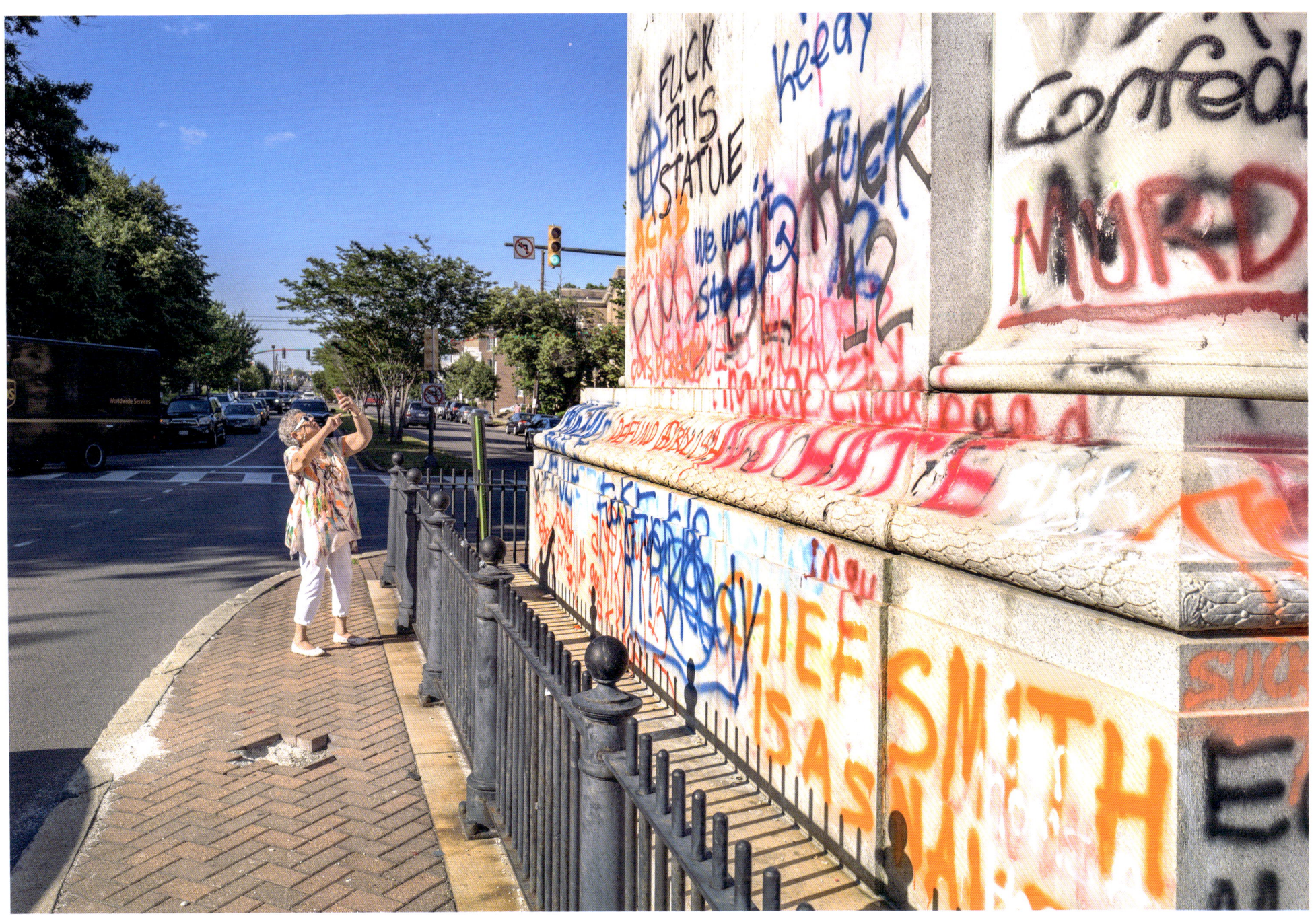

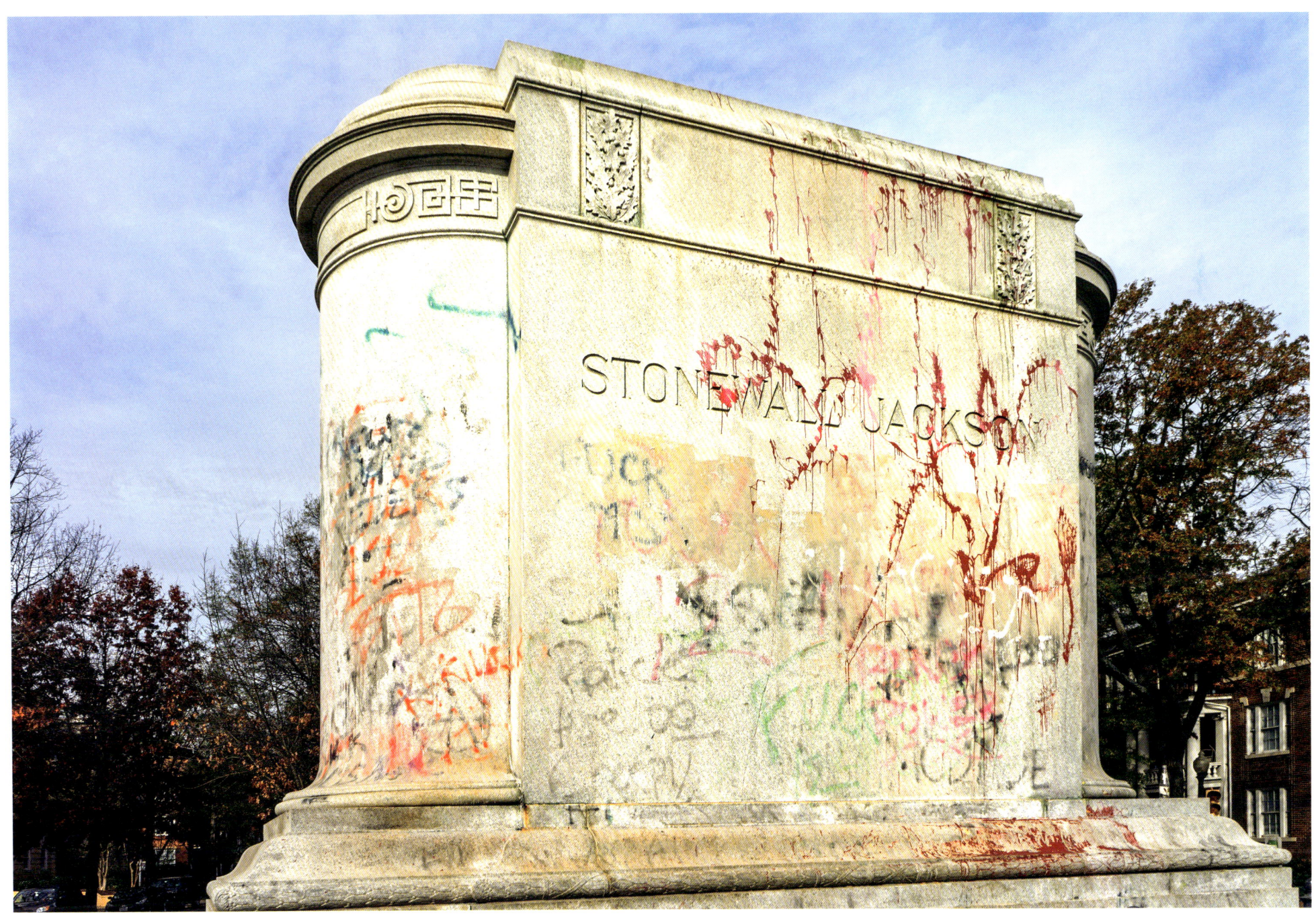

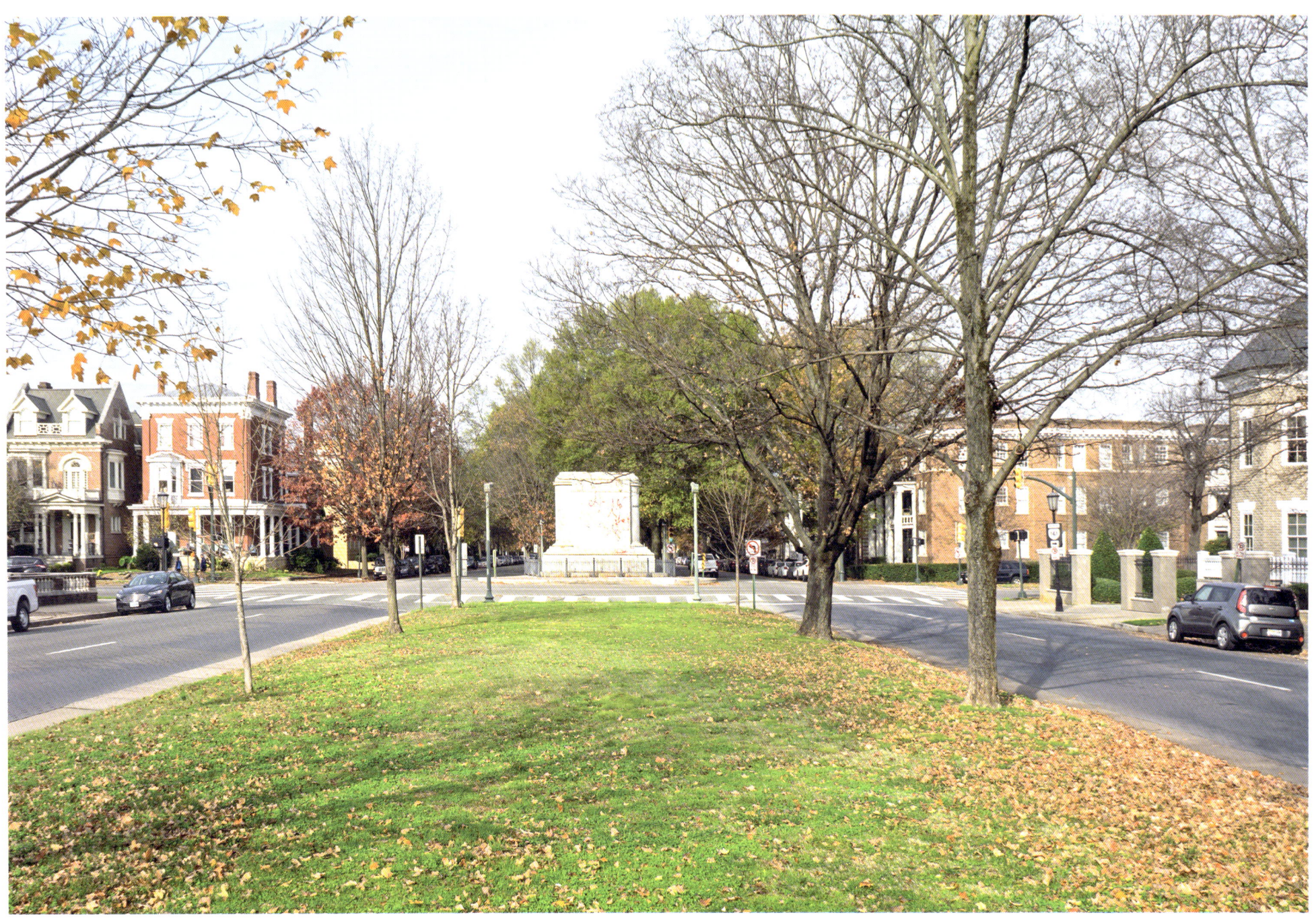

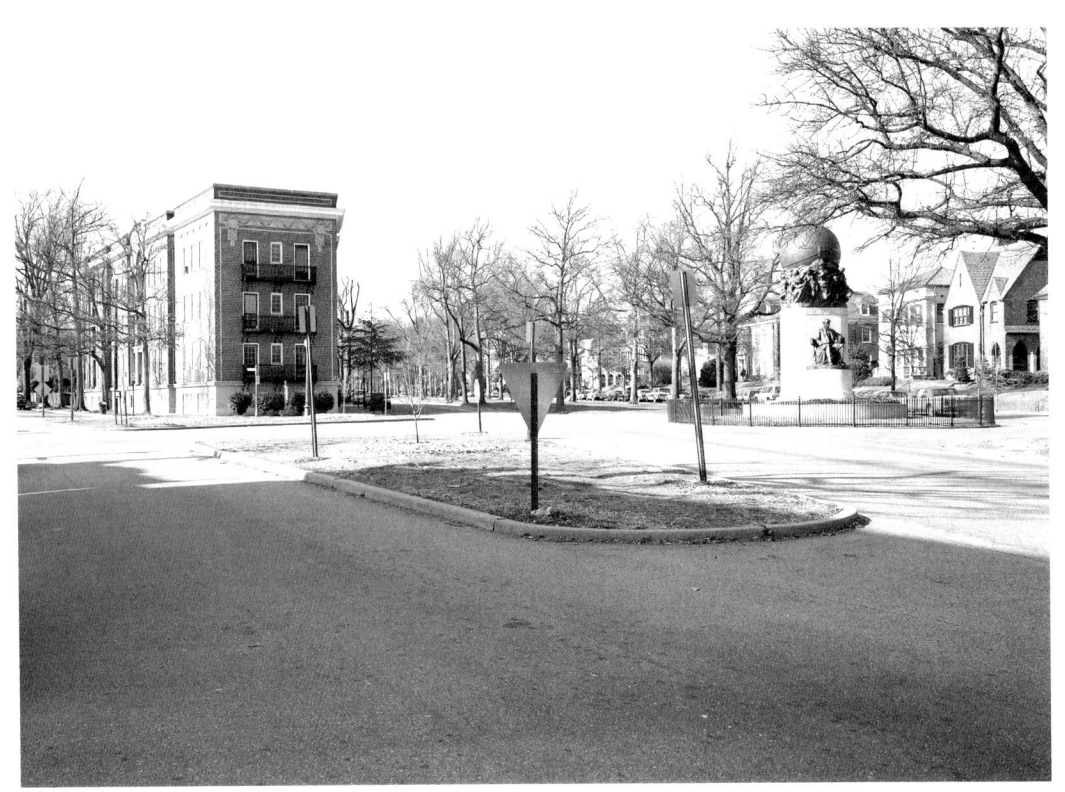

MATTHEW FONTAINE MAURY MONUMENT, 1929

MATTHEW FONTAINE MAURY

He said his mother told him he was named after Fontaine Maury. Growing up, Deane Maury said he knew about his ancestor's contributions to science, especially the contributions to modern oceanography, which earned the man the nickname 'the Pathfinder of Seas.'

What Deane Maury didn't realize until later in life was the role Fontaine Maury played in the Civil War, which included lobbying European countries to support the Confederacy.

'Confederates were treasonous and racists, and believed in a racist cause,' Deane Maury said.

For Deane Maury, he said though everyone in his family may not share his opinion, he believes the predominant view is in line with his. 'The hard fact is he made the wrong moral choice in the most critical part of his life,' Deane Maury said of his ancestor.

Mike Murillo
WTOP
2 July 2020

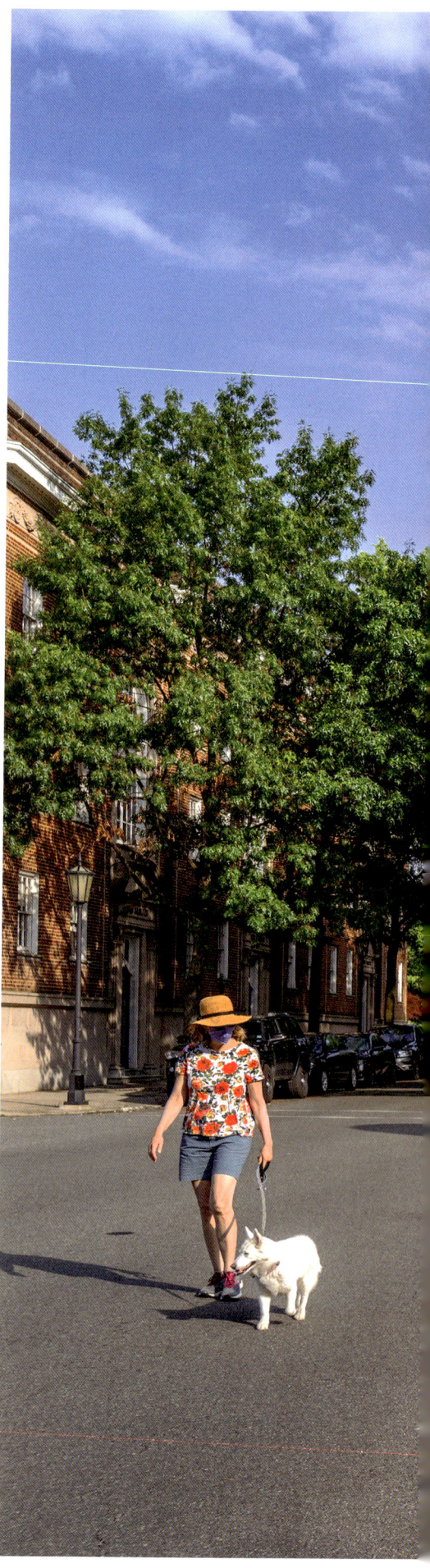

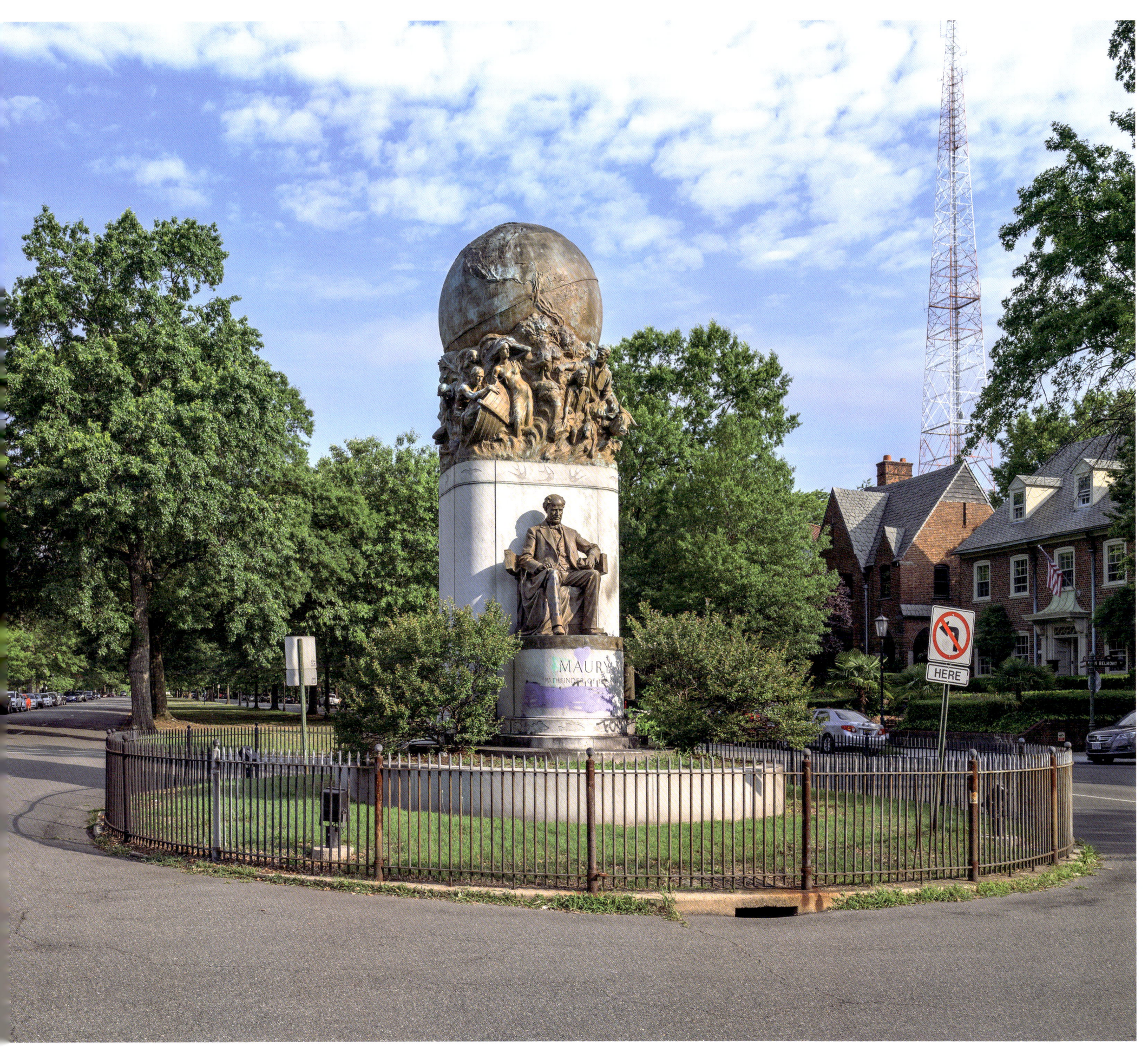

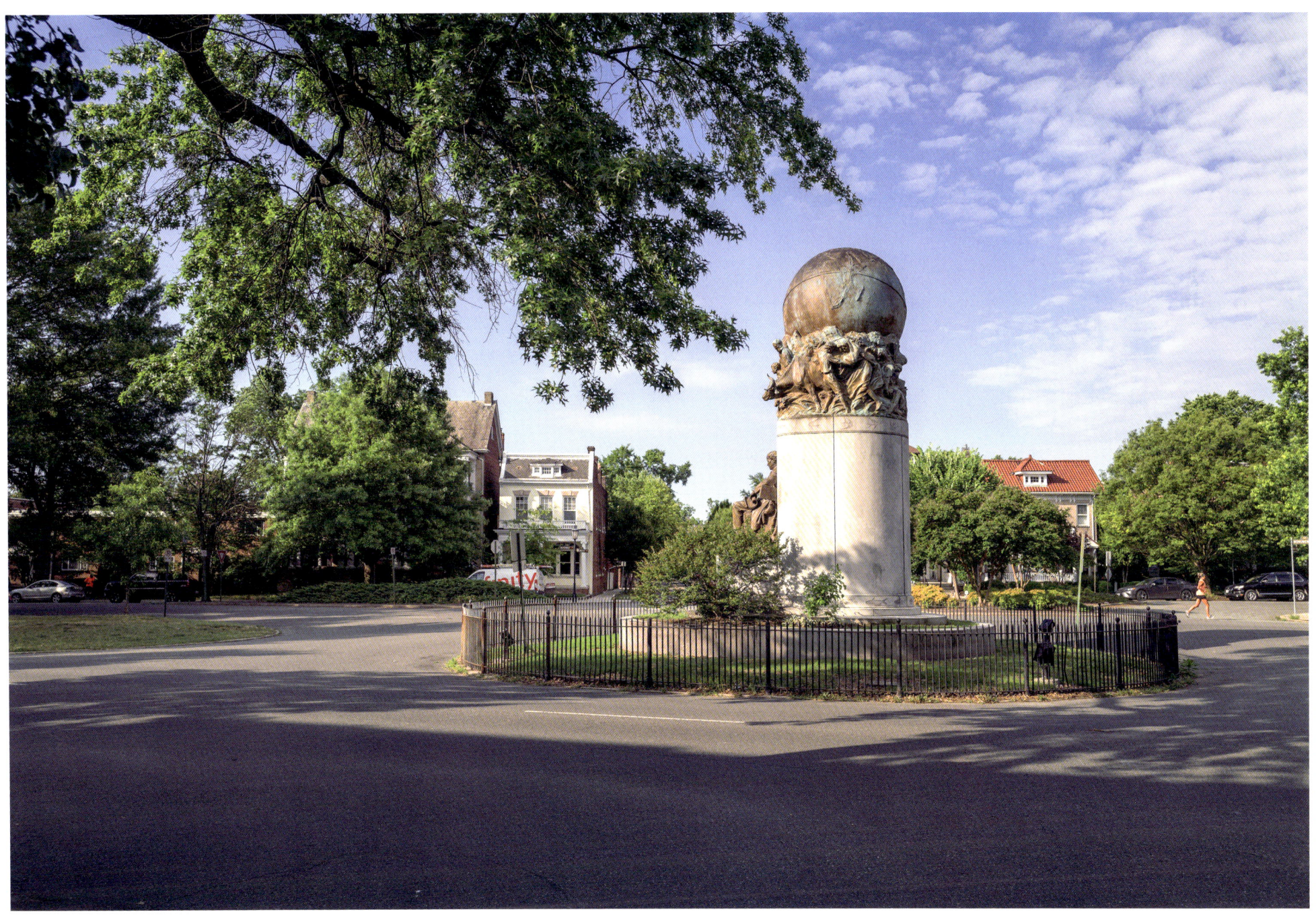

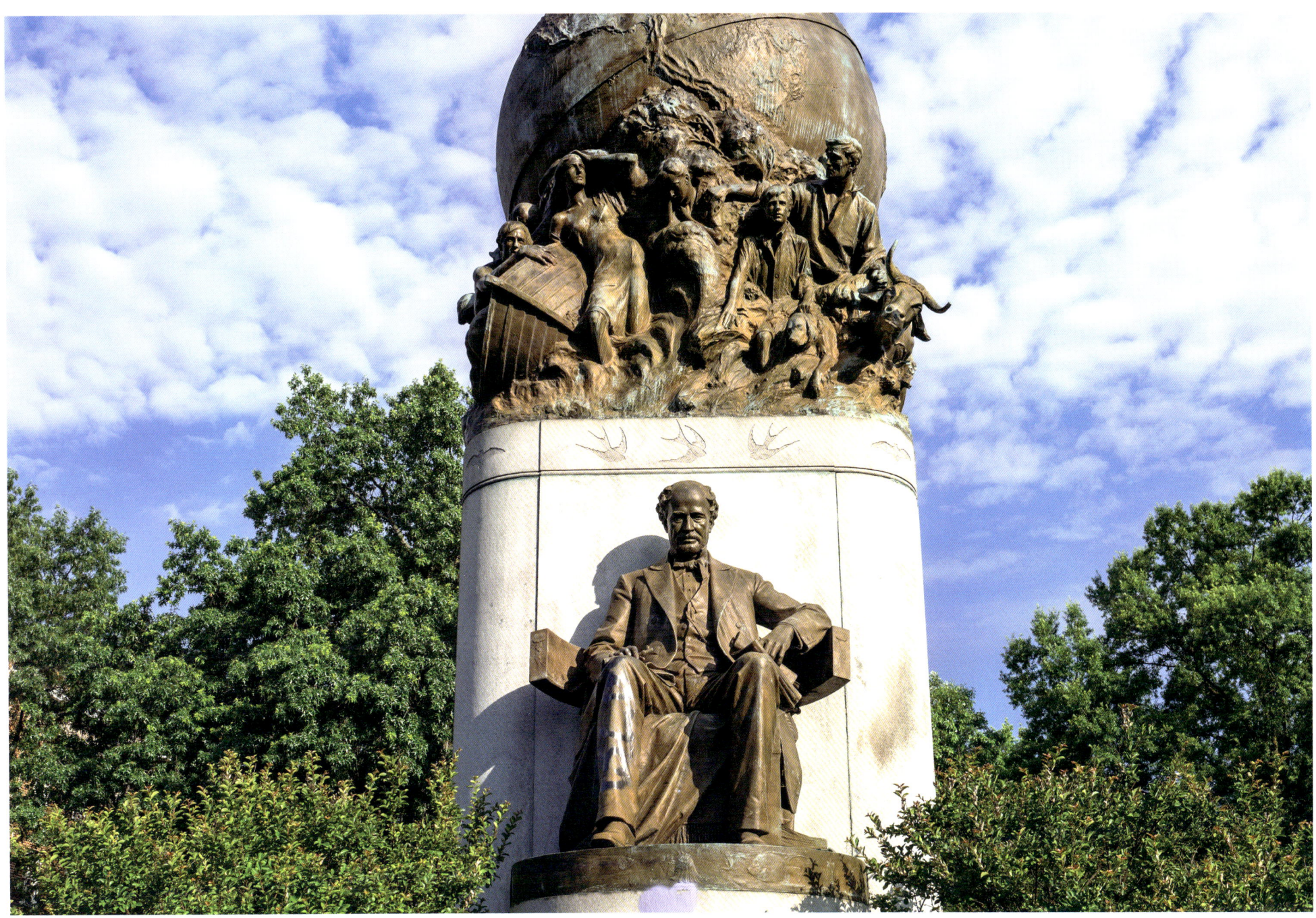

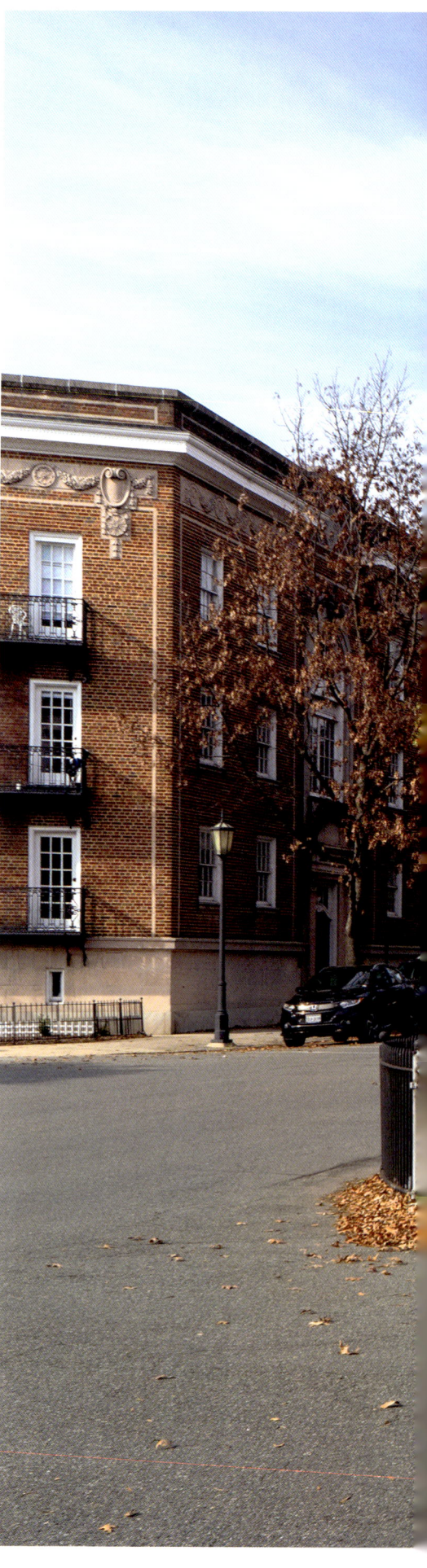

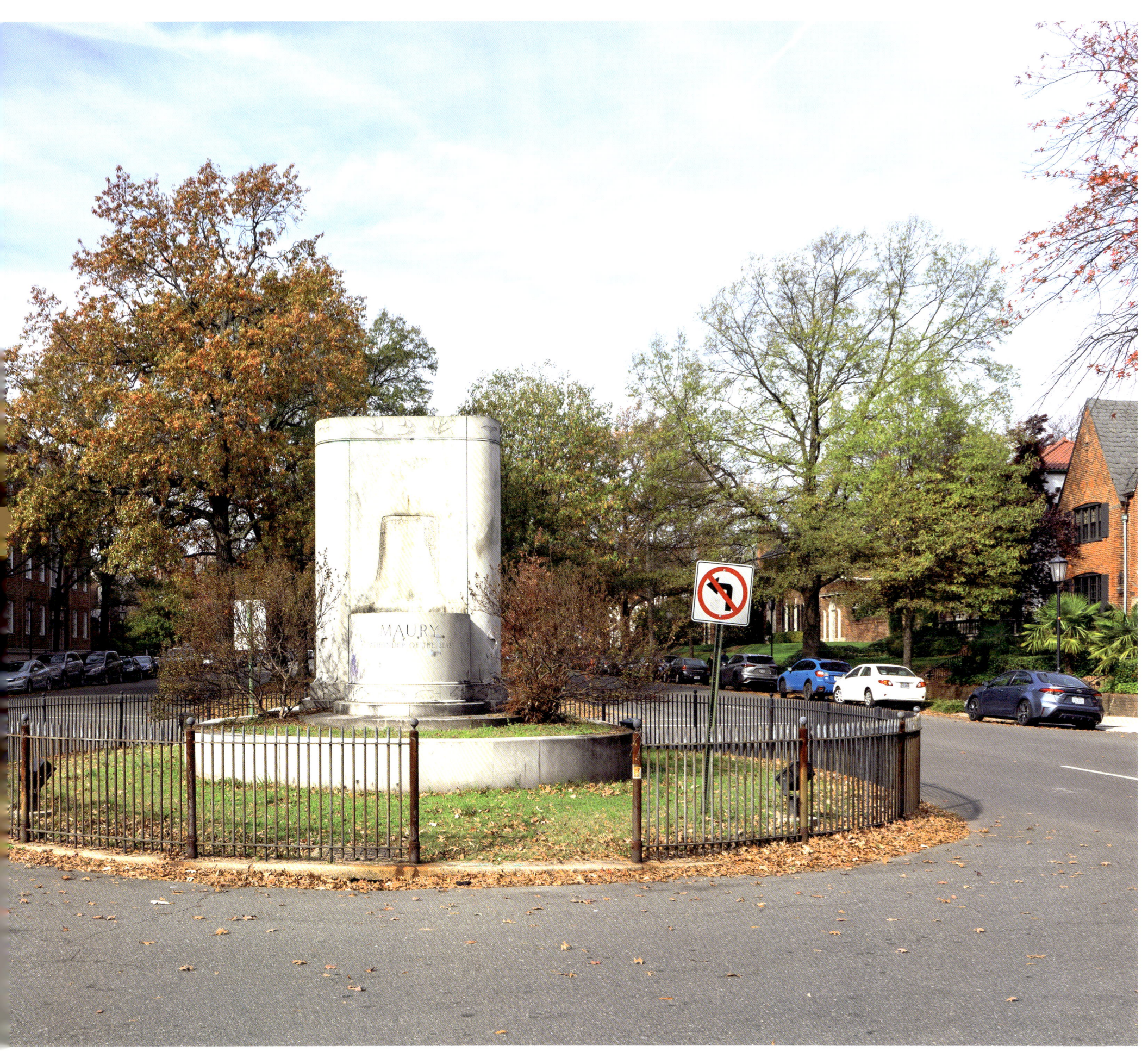

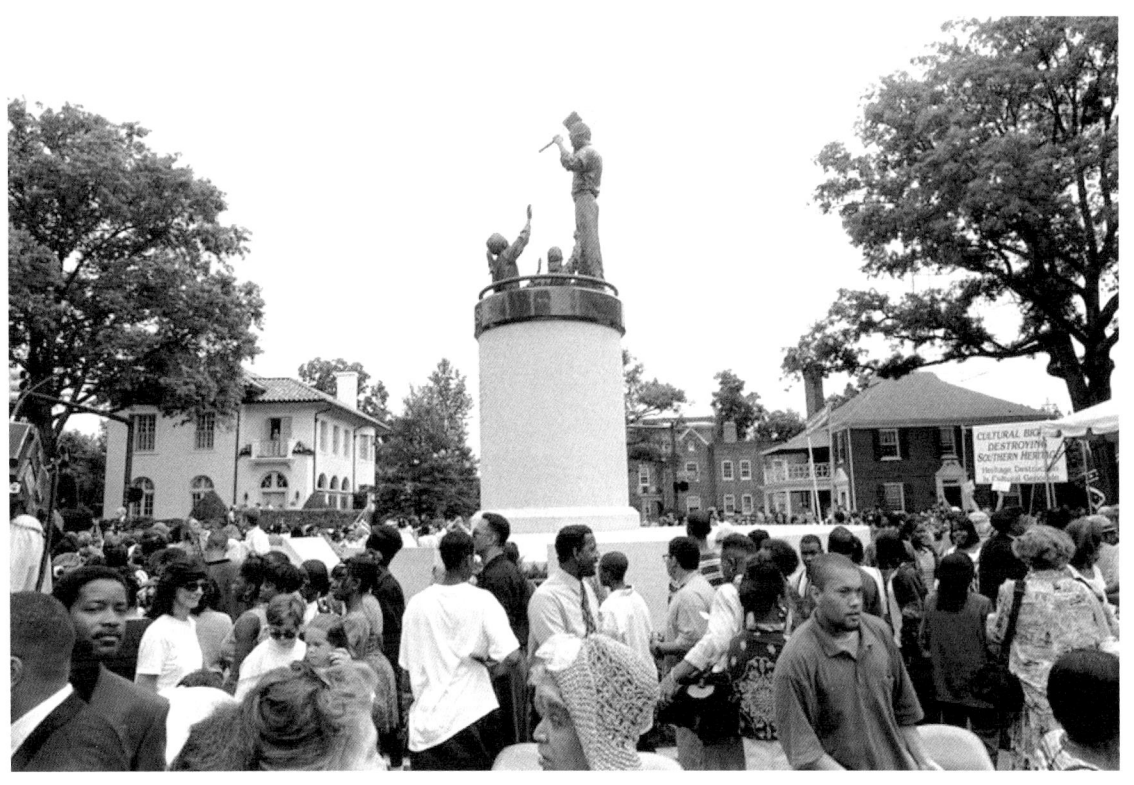

ARTHUR ASHE MONUMENT, 1996

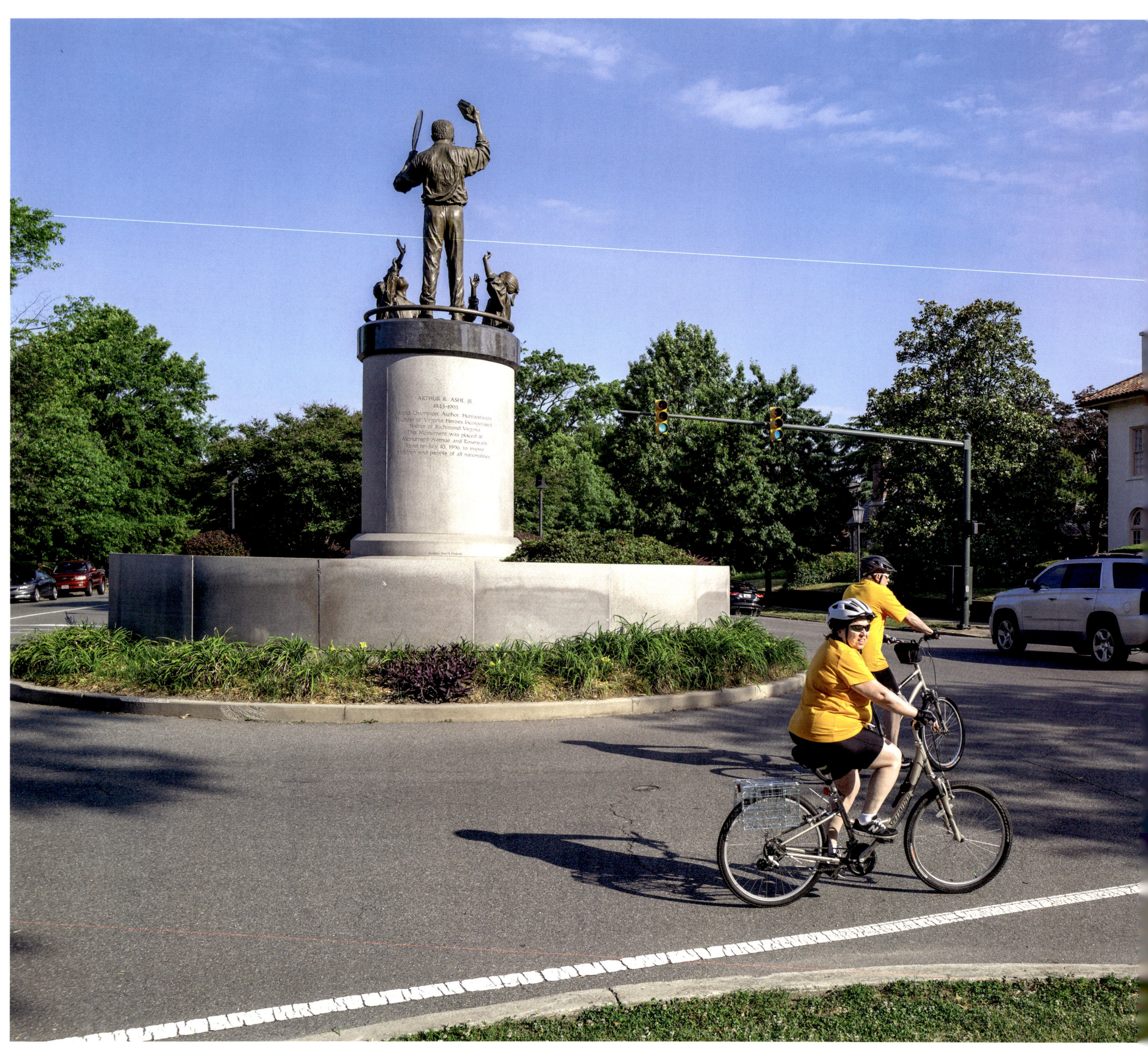

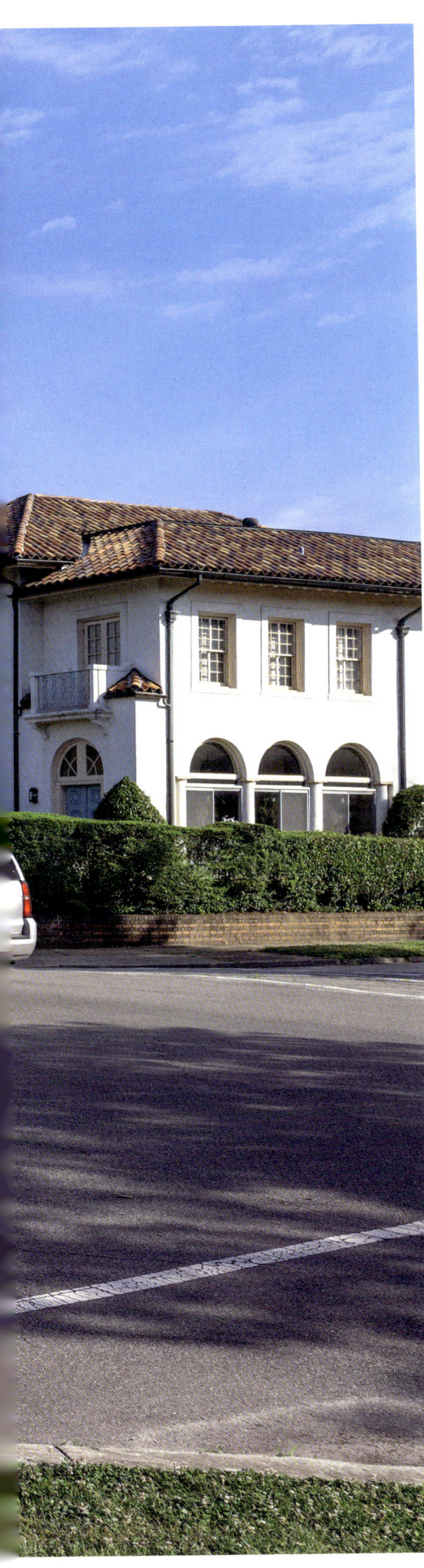

ARTHUR ASHE

With the pull of a cord that unveiled a statue of hometown hero Arthur Ashe Jr., the Confederate capital's landmark thoroughfare was transformed today from a period piece to what former governor L. Douglas Wilder proclaimed as 'an avenue for all people.'

Ashe, who learned to play tennis on the city's segregated playgrounds and rose to become Wimbledon's first black champion and an eloquent writer and spokesman for education and equal rights, took his place among the Confederate icons memorialized on Monument Avenue: Robert E. Lee, Thomas J. 'Stonewall' Jackson and other lights of the Lost Cause.

Donald P. Baker
The Washington Post
11 July 1996

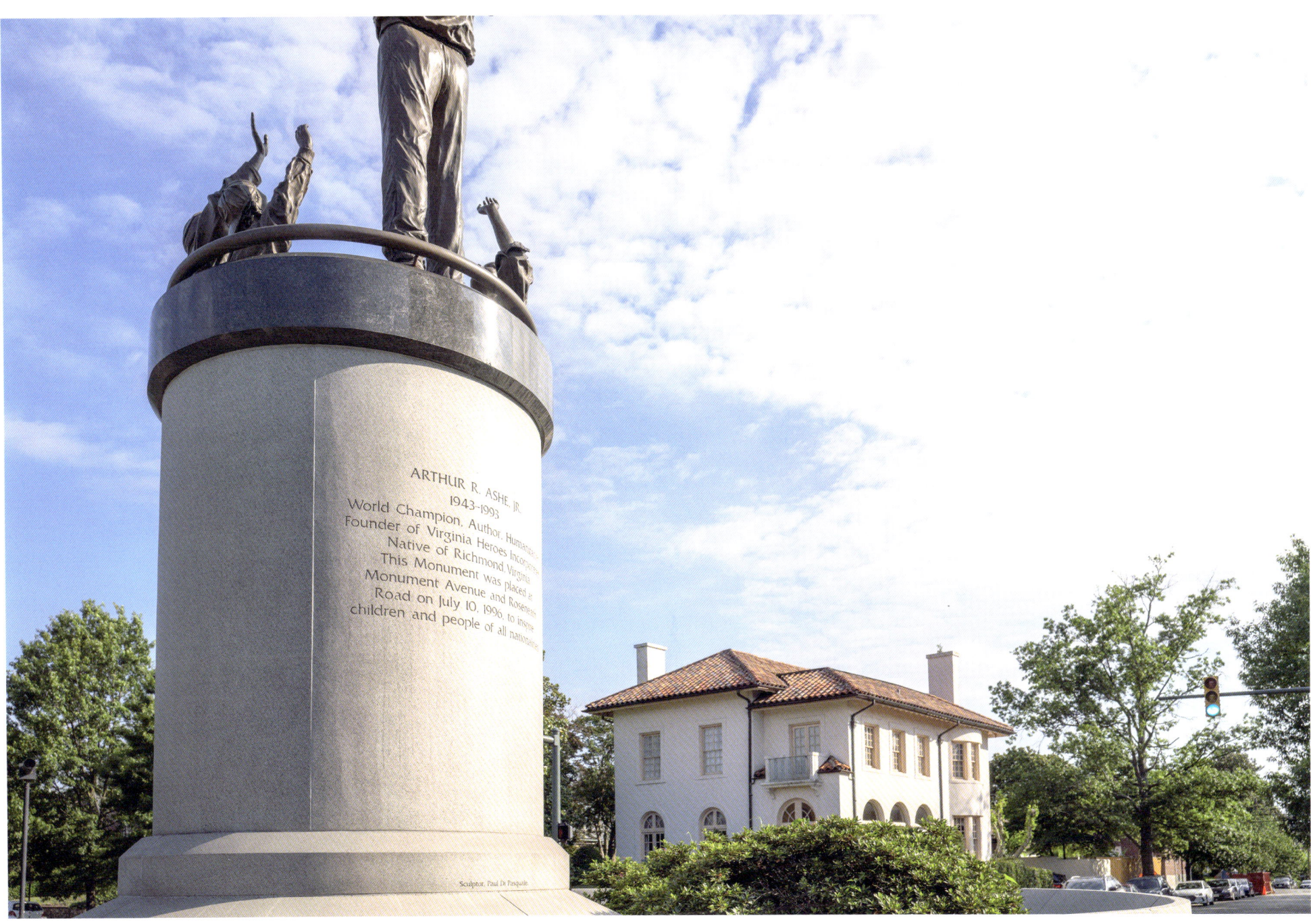

ARTHUR R. ASHE, JR.
1943-1993
World Champion, Author, Humanitarian
Founder of Virginia Heroes Incorporated
Native of Richmond, Virginia
This Monument was placed at
Monument Avenue and Roseneath
Road on July 10, 1996, to inspire
children and people of all nationalities

Sculptor, Paul Di Pasquale

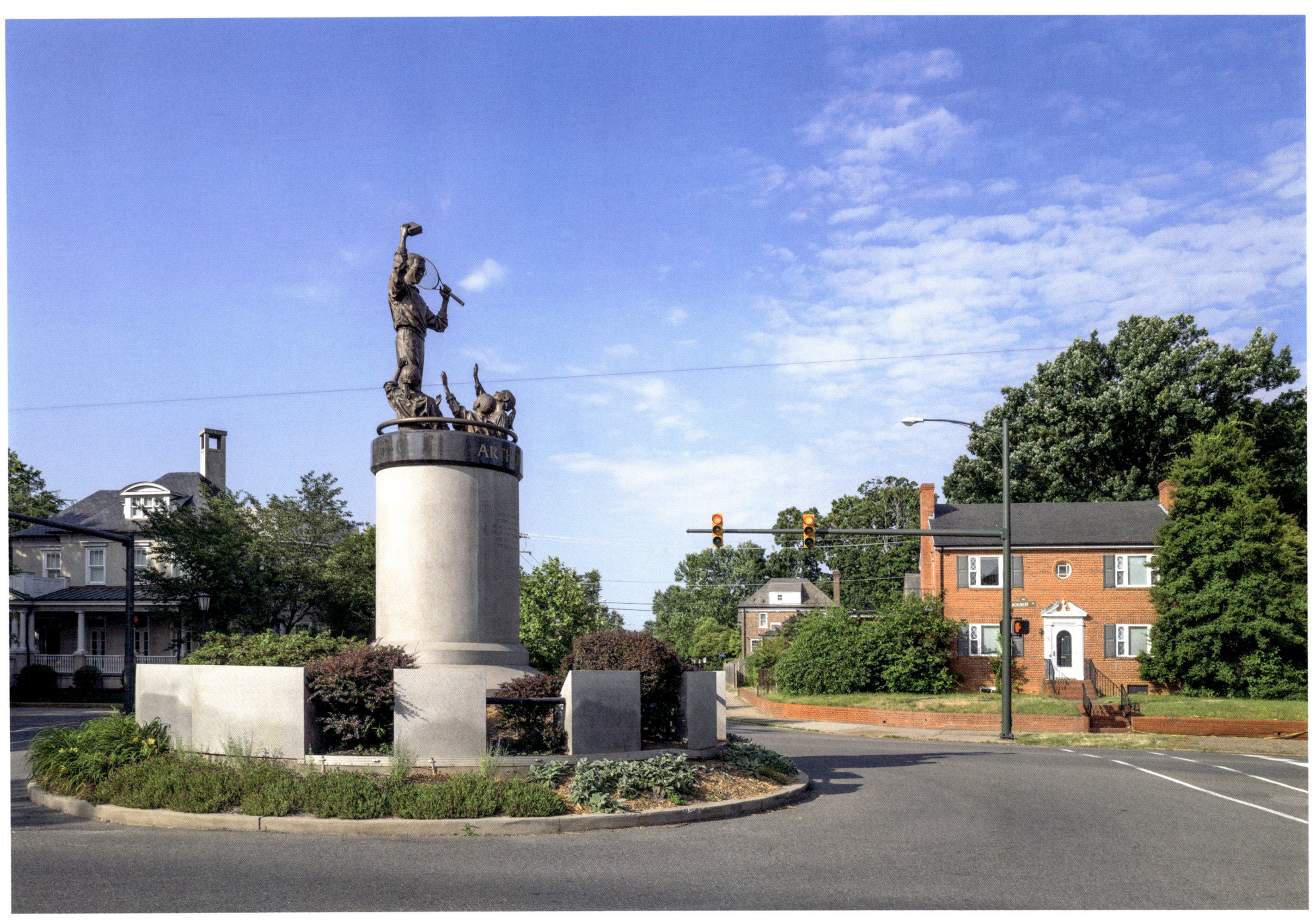

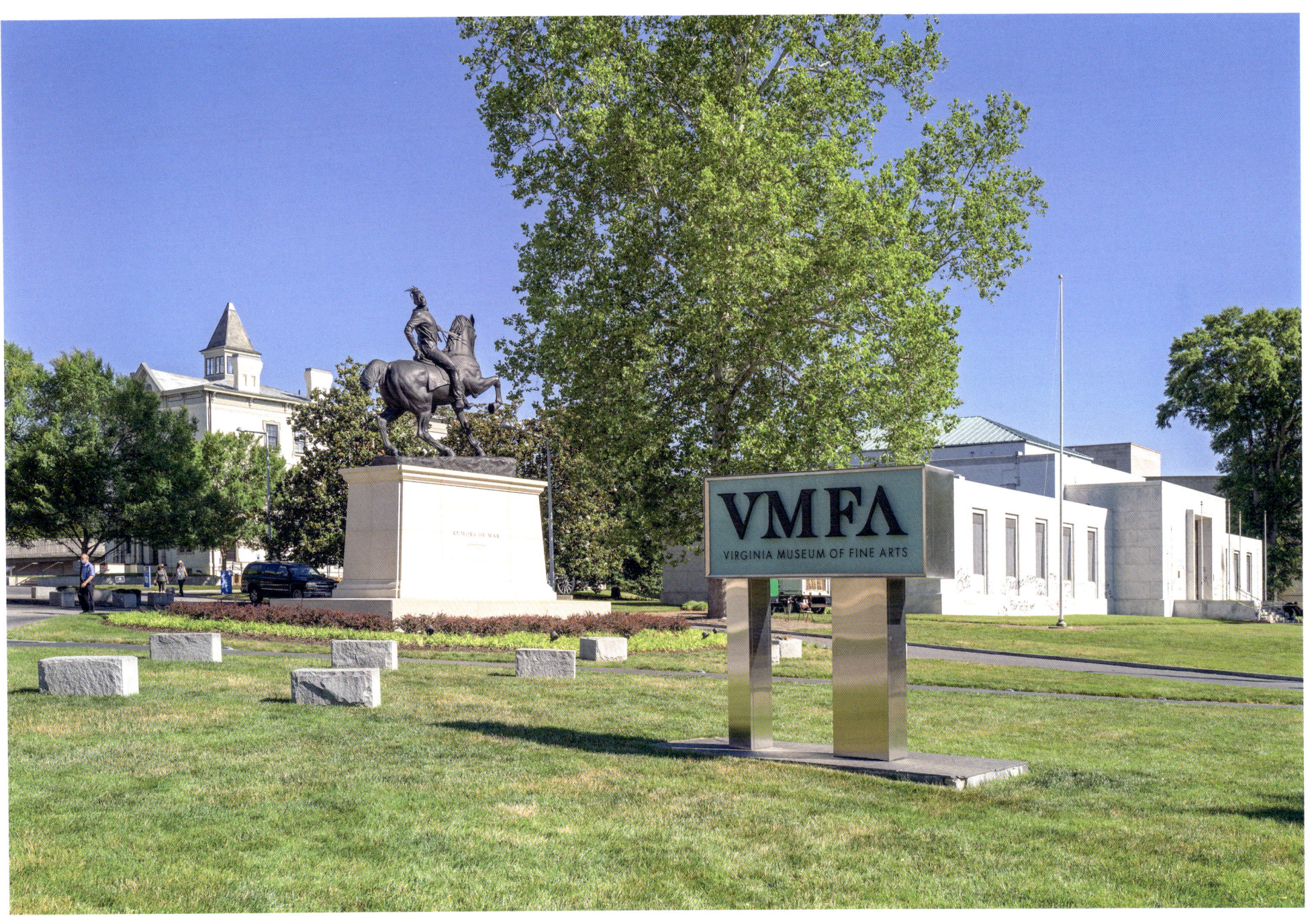

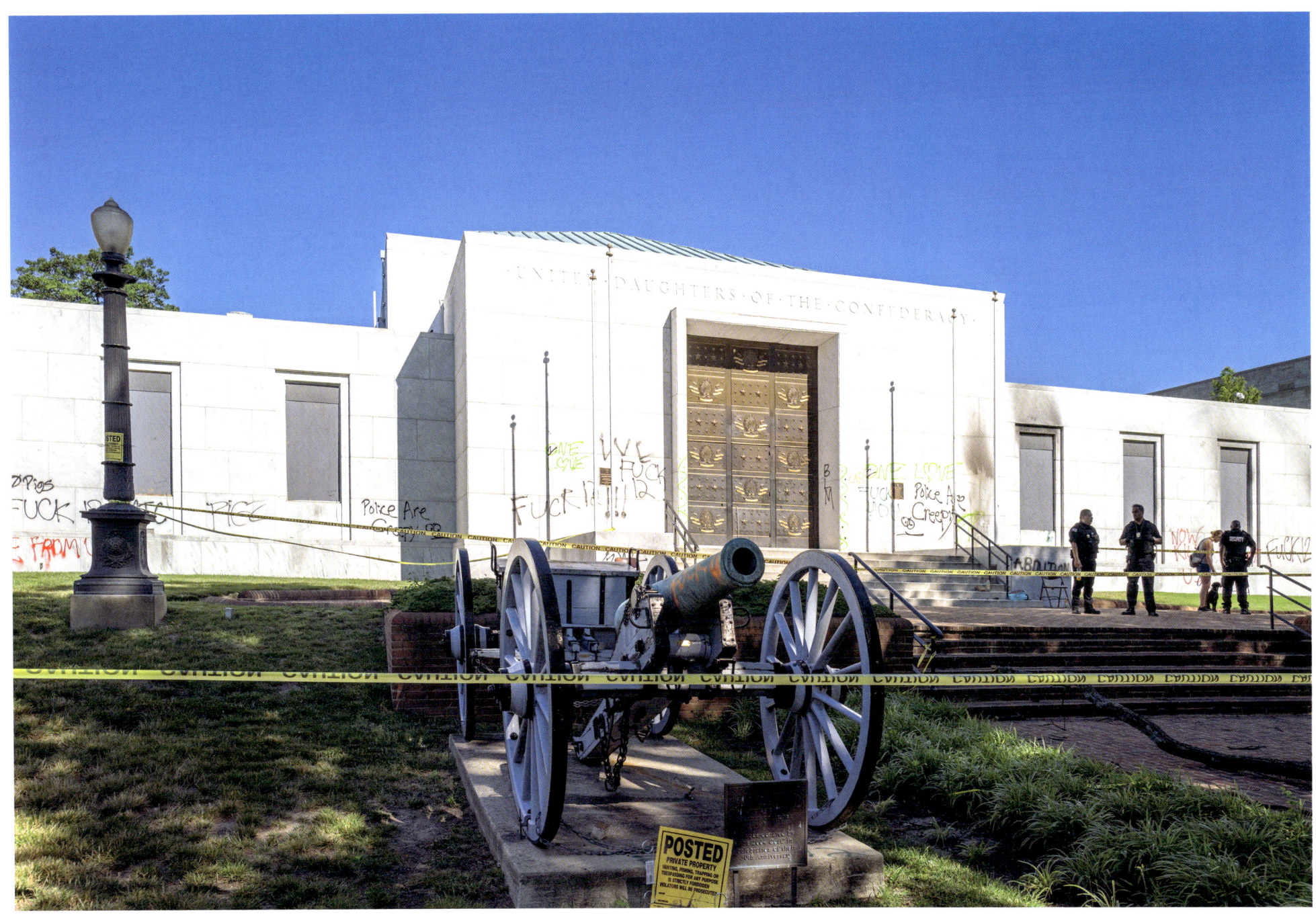

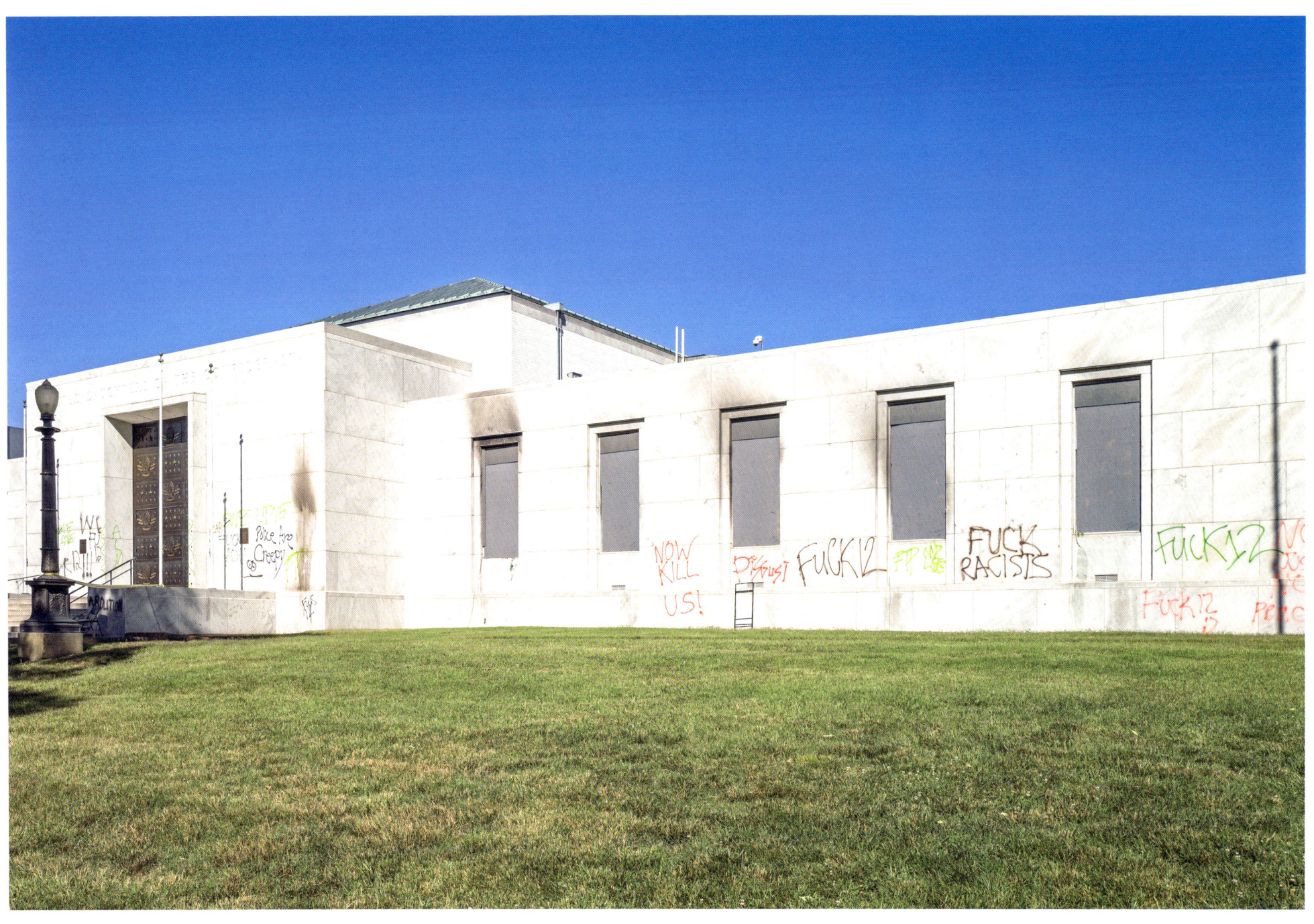

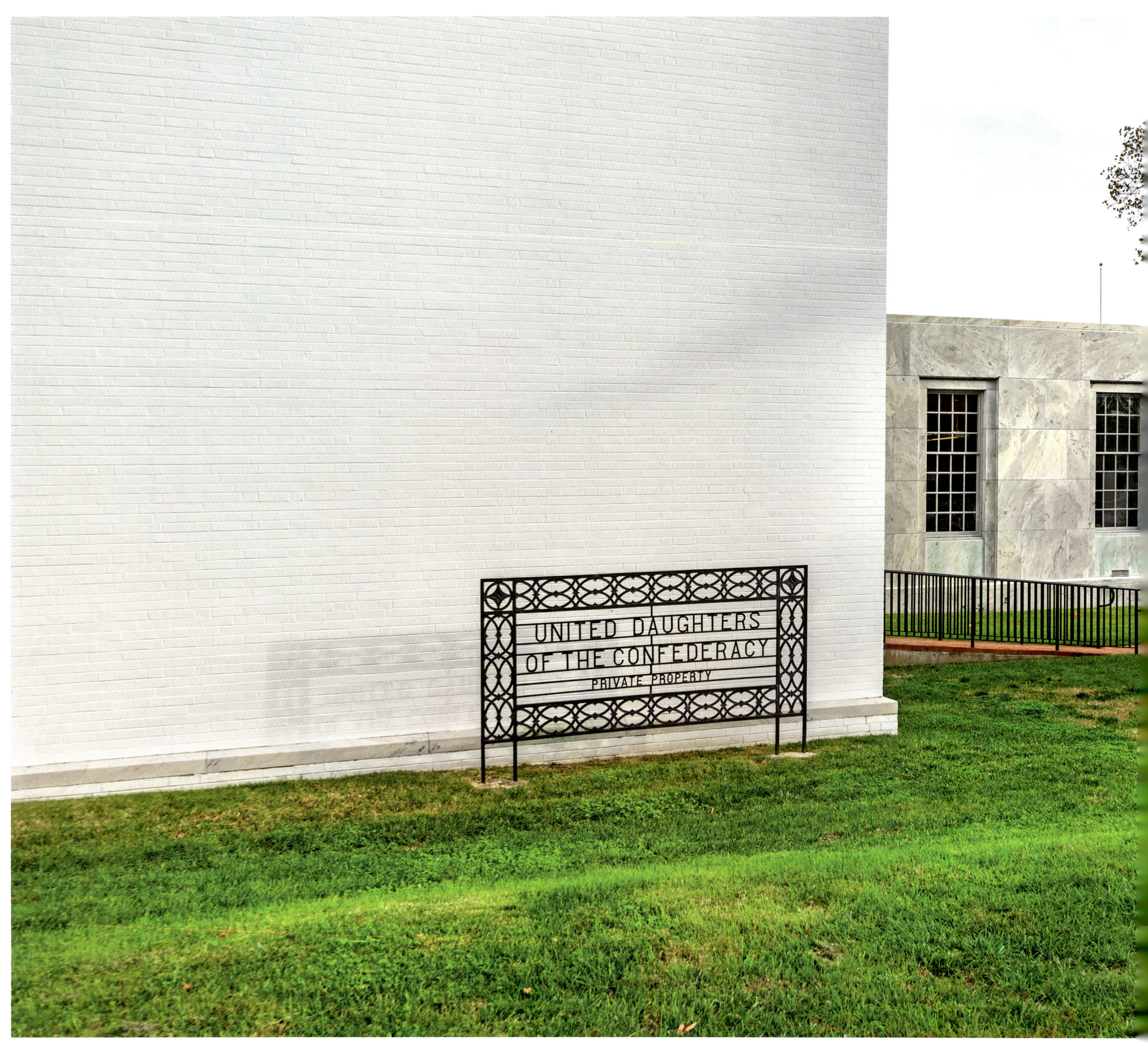

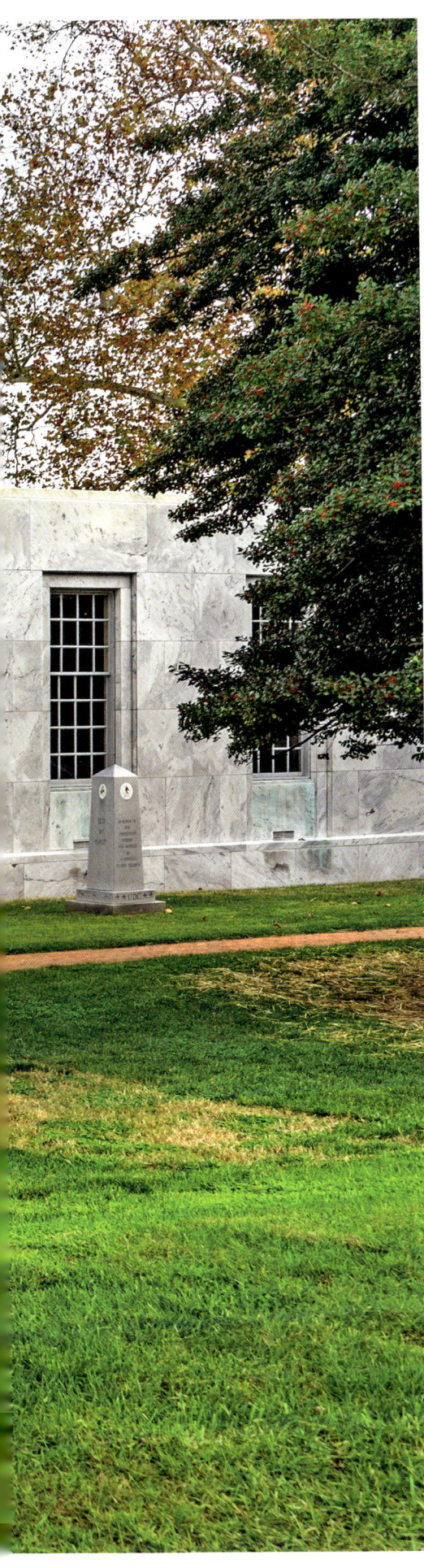

UNITED DAUGHTERS OF THE CONFEDERACY

While not a statue, the UDC headquarters functions as a Confederate monument because it represents the very organization responsible for the vast majority of statues to the Confederacy throughout the South and, in some cases, even outside the region. That it was attacked by protesters who also targeted the Lee Memorial suggests that local activists understood the building to be as offensive as a traditional monument.

Founded in 1894, the UDC, also known as the Daughters, quickly became the most popular of all southern white women's organizations with a membership – drawn mainly from the middle and upper classes – that peaked at 100,000 at the beginning of World War I. The UDC's members rapidly became leaders of the 'Lost Cause' interpretation of the Civil War – which recalled Confederate defeat as a 'just cause' while also dismissing slavery as a central issue of the Civil War.

Karen L. Cox
Perspectives on History
August 6 2020

RUMORS OF WAR

On Tuesday, (Kehinde) Wiley was greeted by the throng of Richmonders like a rock star. Wearing a colorful African-print suit and Converse sneakers, and with his mother sitting in the front row, Wiley spoke of the Monument Avenue figures that inspired him.

'I saw some extraordinary sculpture. People took a lot of time to make something powerful. Beautiful. Elegant. Menacing,' he said. 'We can do better.'

Now, he said, is a time to appropriate the images of the past and update them for a new era. 'There's something moving in the culture. There something changing in the winds,' he said. 'I'm tired of the dysfunction; I'm tired of the strife.'

Gregory S. Schneider
The Washington Post
11 December 2019

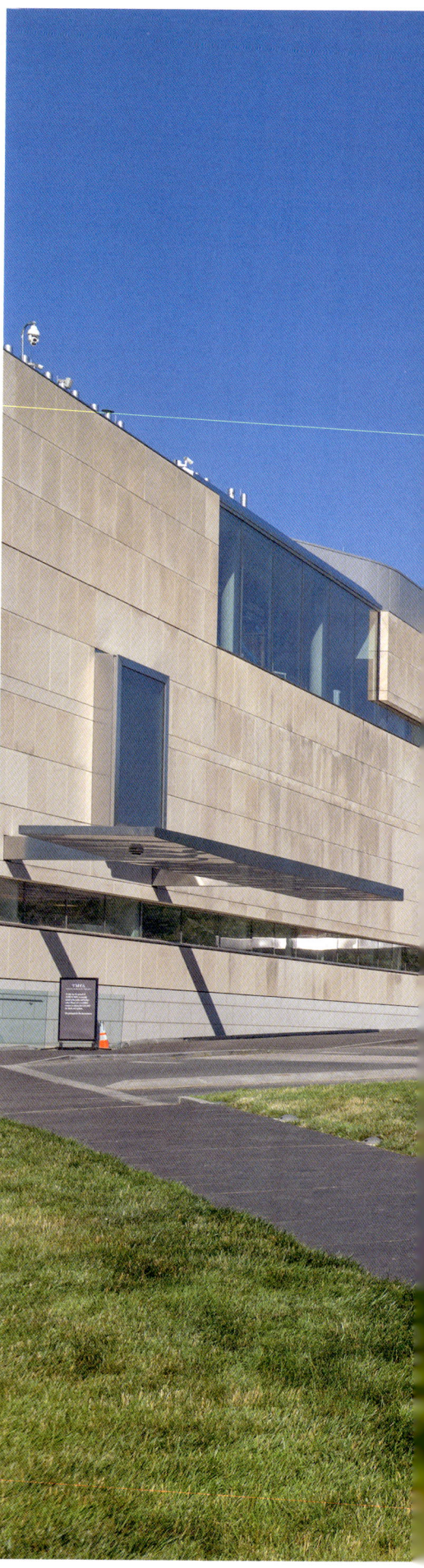

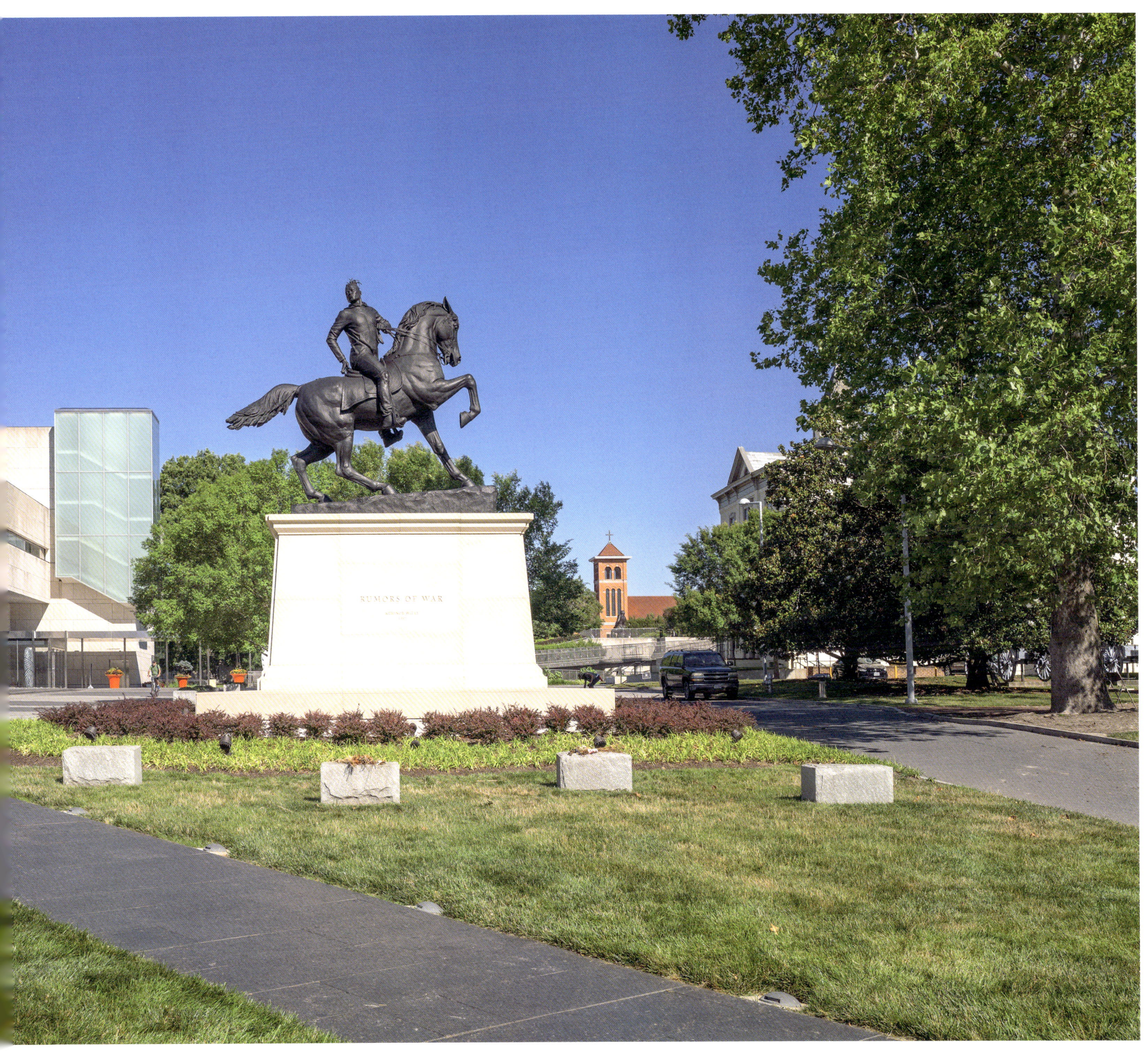

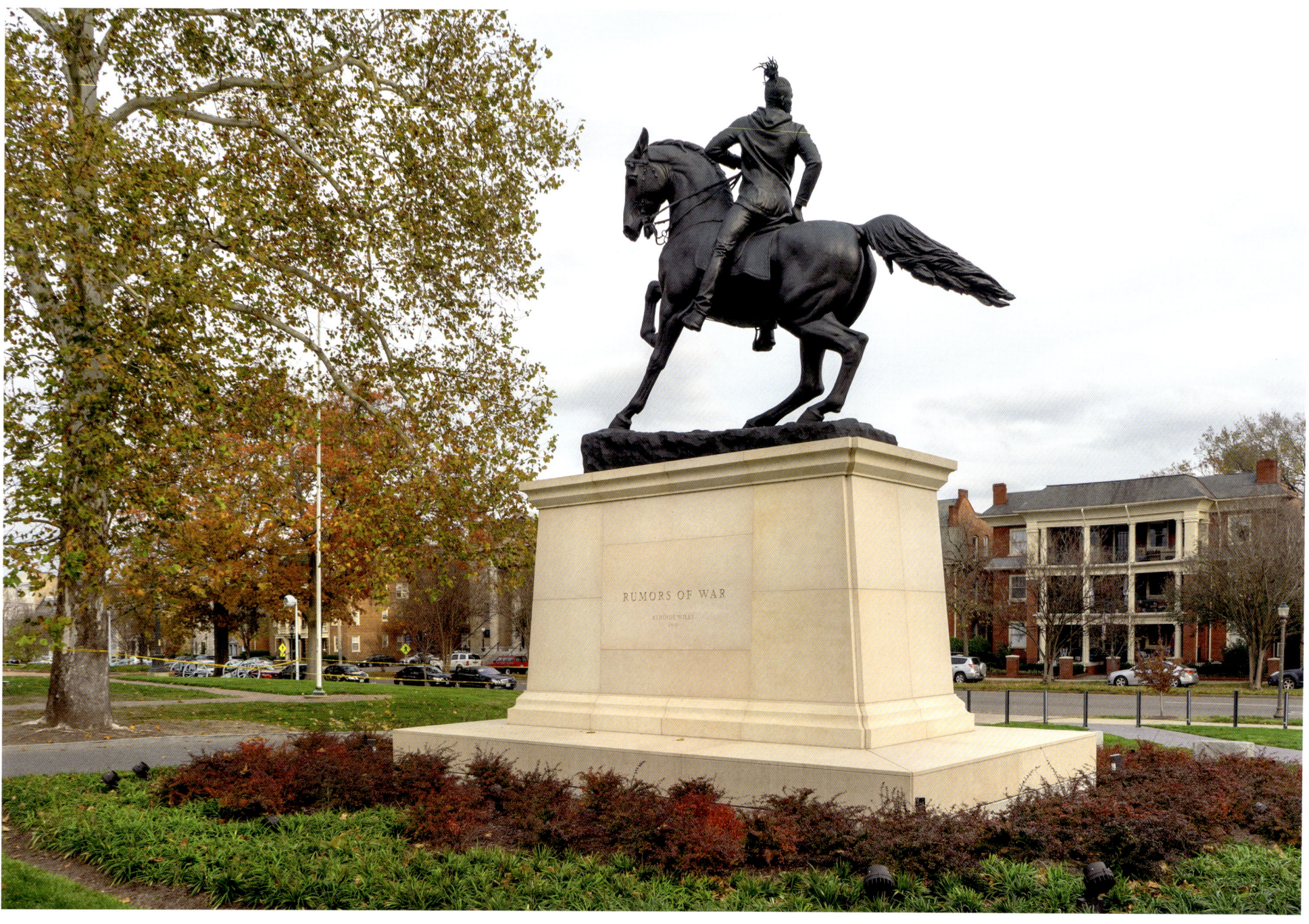

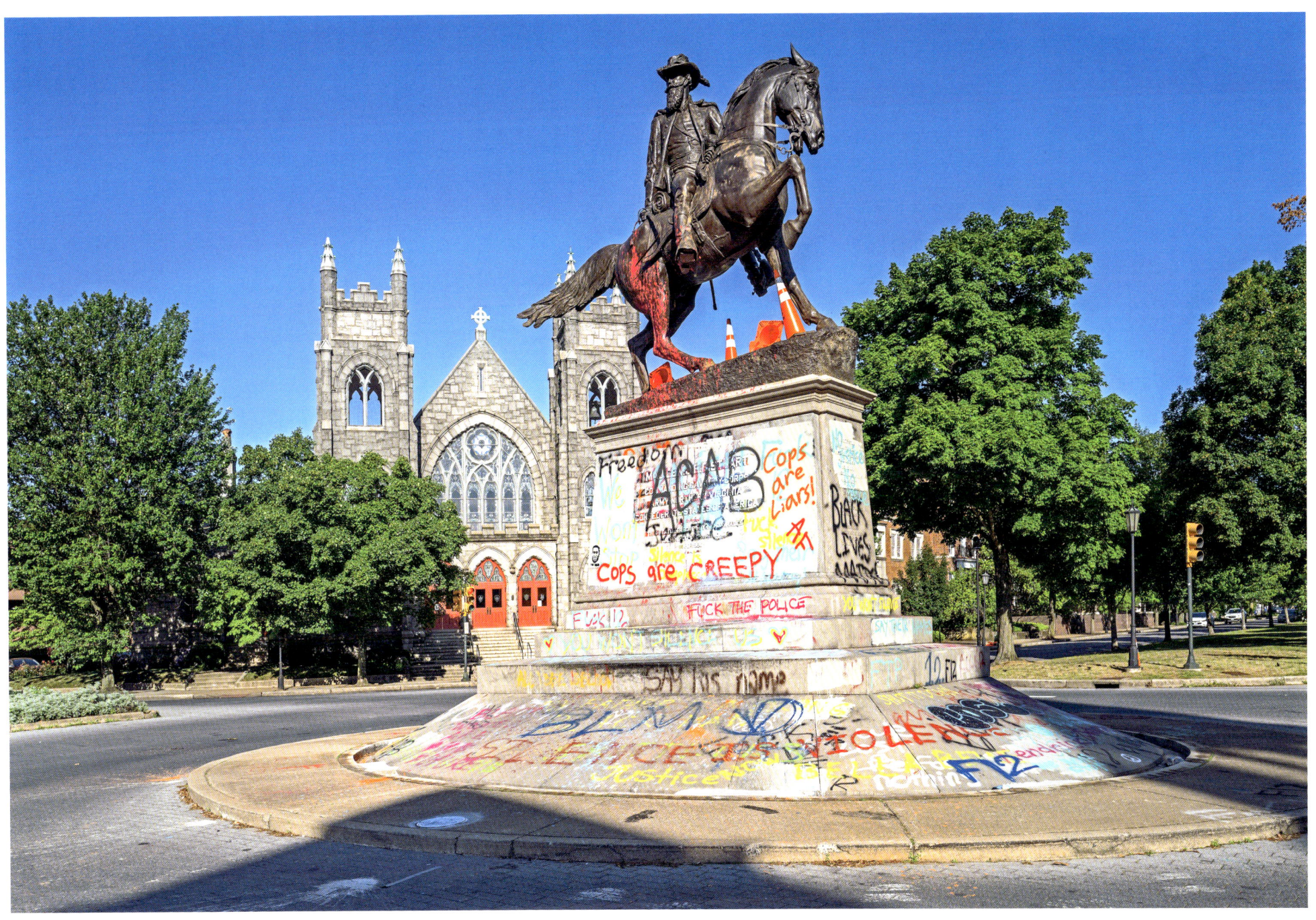

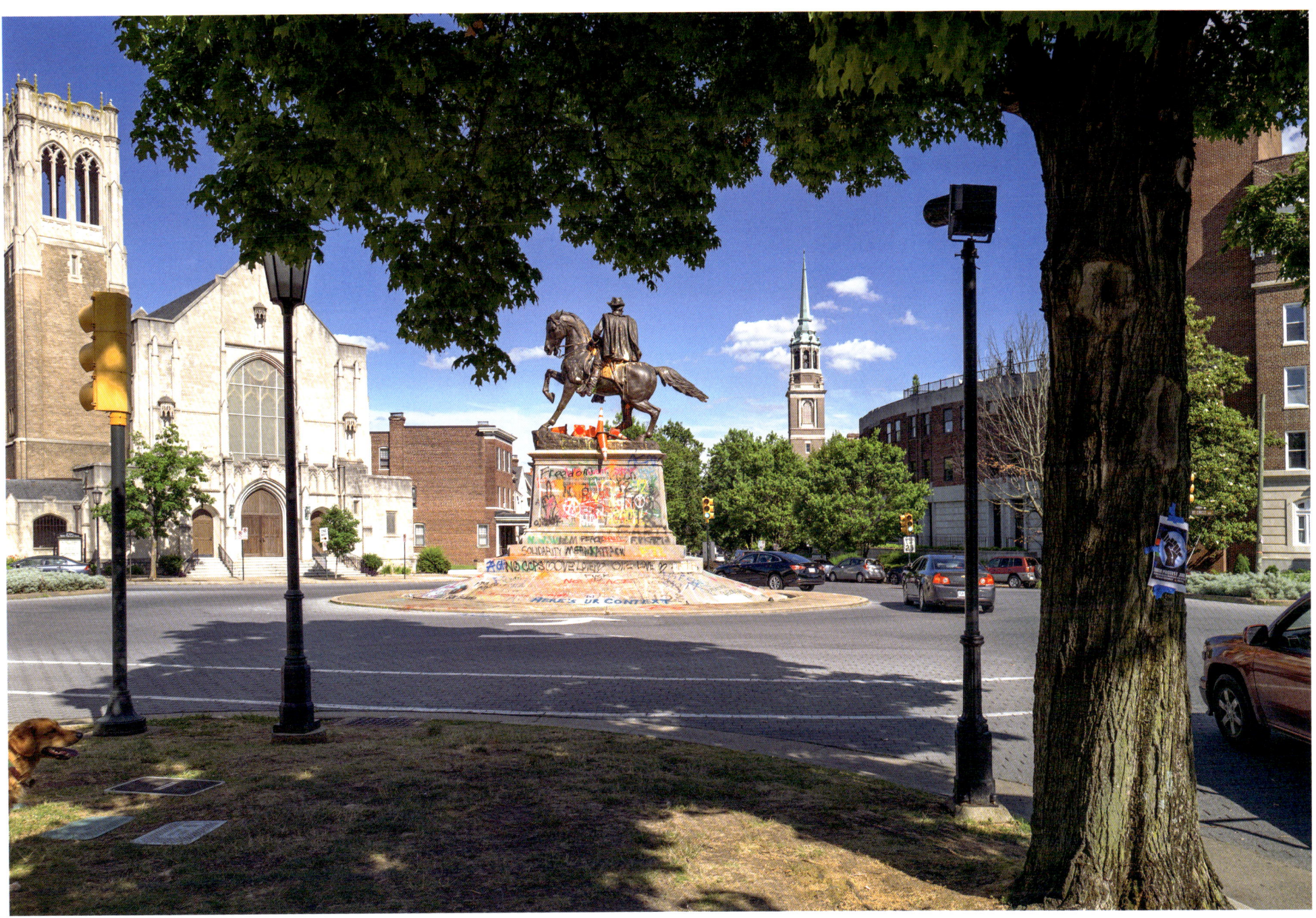

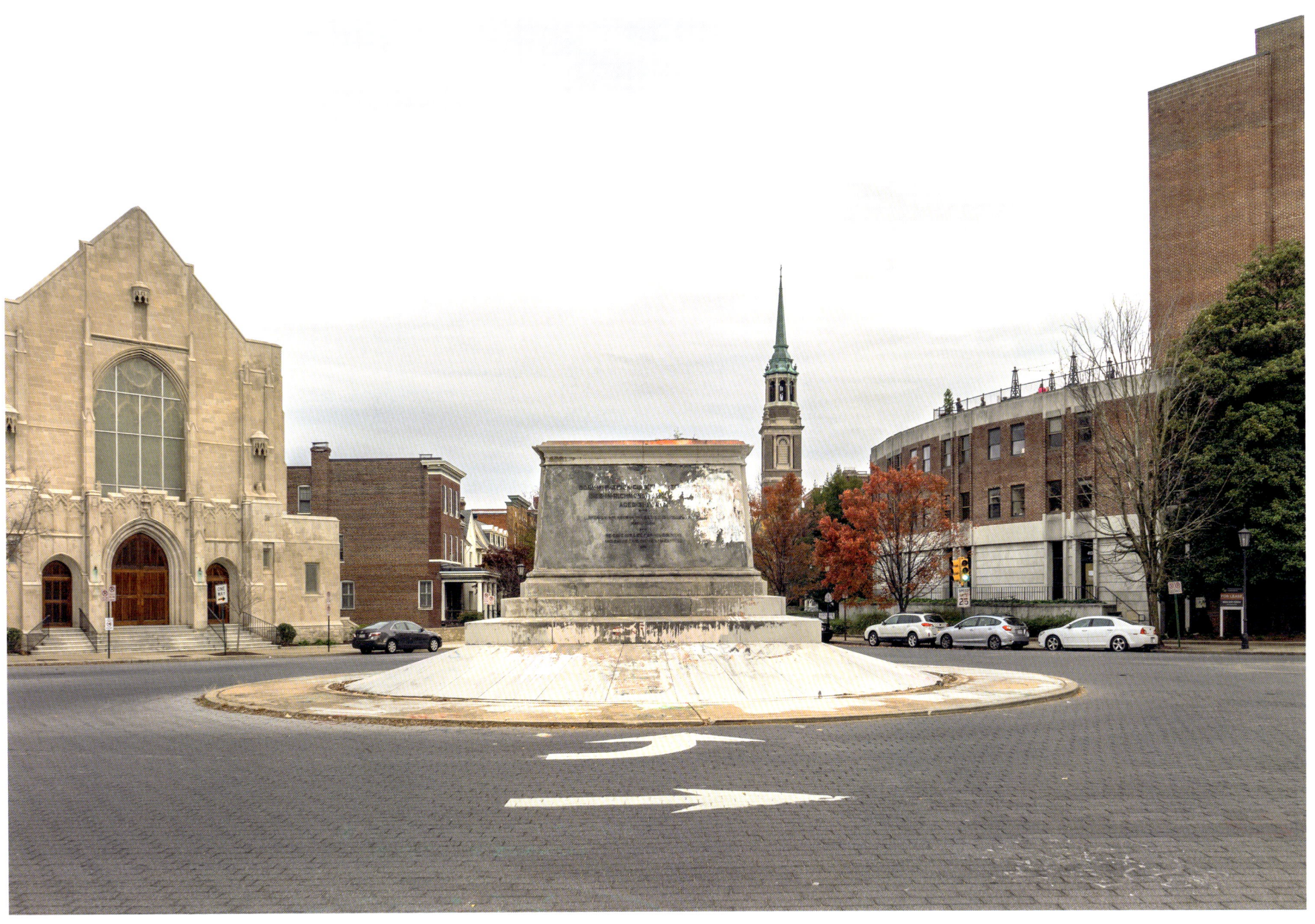

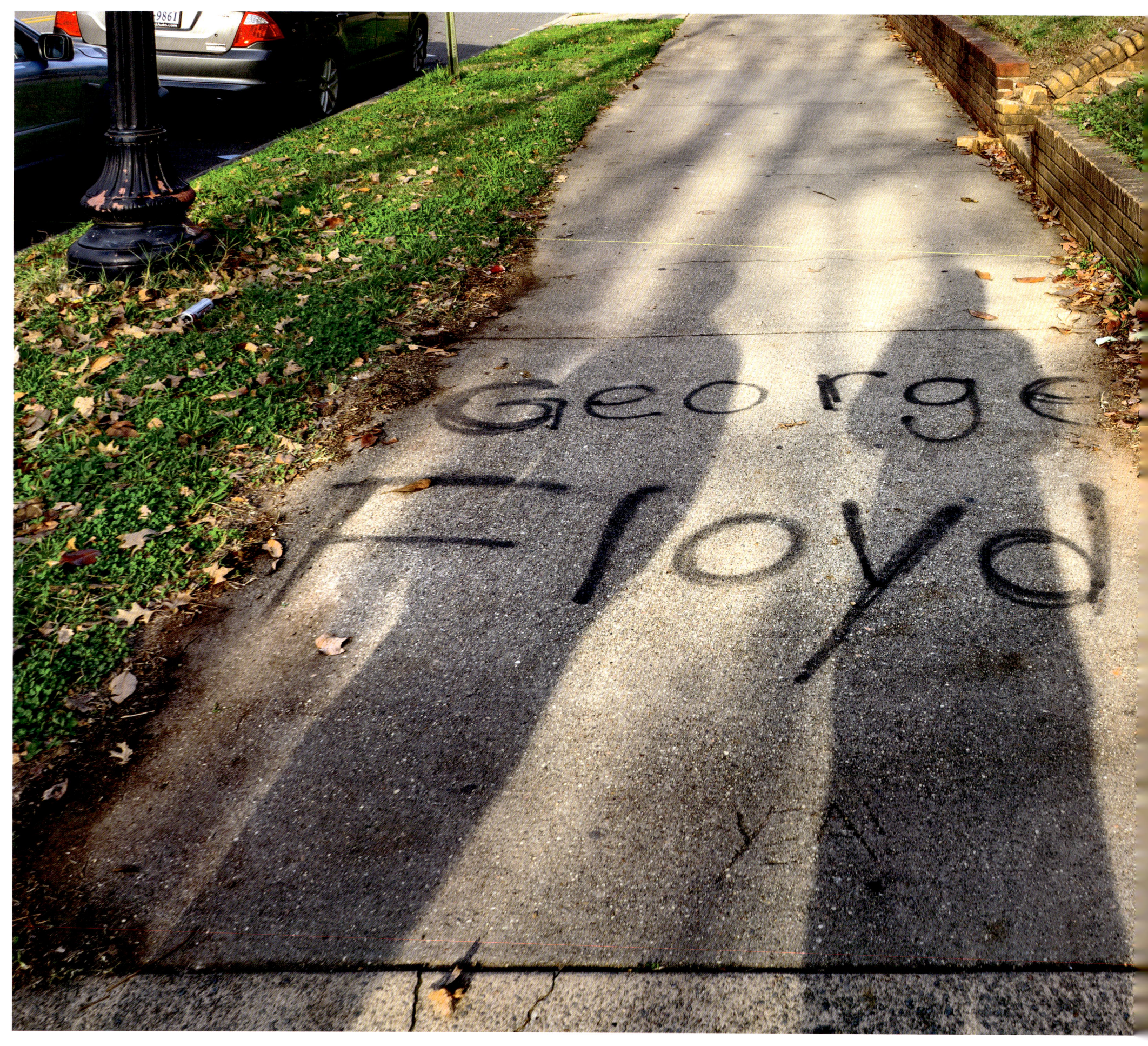

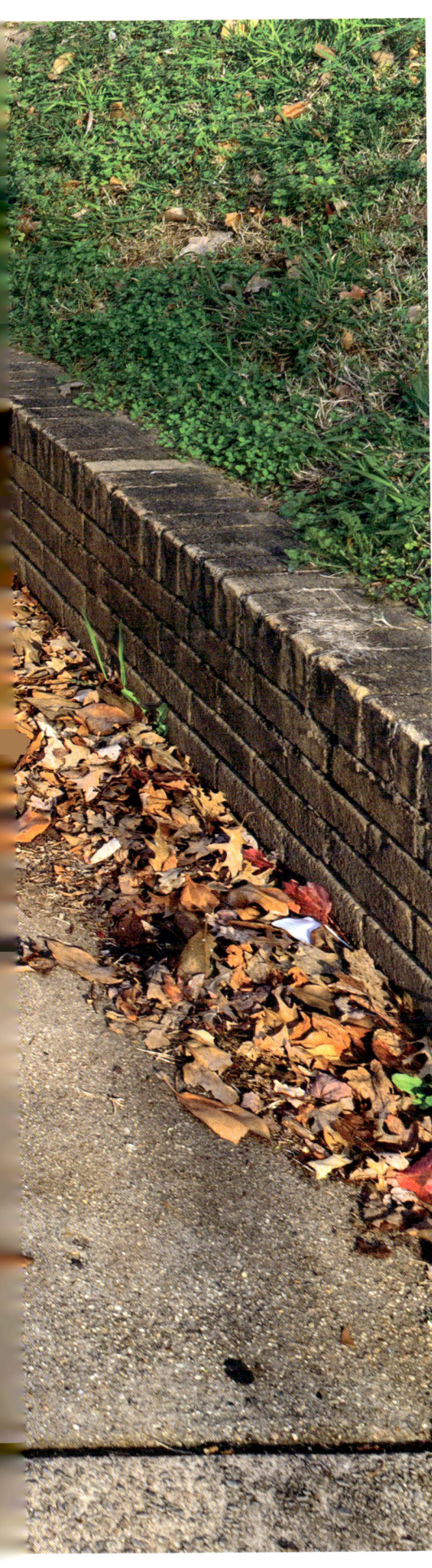

CONFEDERATE MONUMENTS

The most terrible thing about war, I am convinced, is the monuments – the awful things we are compelled to build in order to remember the victims. In the South, particularly, human ingenuity has been put to it to explain the Confederacy on its war monuments. Of course, the plain truth of the matter would be an inscription something like this: 'Sacred to the memory of those who fought to Perpetuate Human Slavery.'

W.E.B. Du Bois
1931

Brian Rose studied at Cooper Union with photographers Joel Meyerowitz and Larry Fink. His documentation of Lower Manhattan over a twenty-year period resulted in three books – *Time and Space on the Lower East Side*, *Metamorphosis*, and *WTC*, a chronicle of the Twin Towers and the rebuilding of the World Trade Center. His study of Berlin after the fall of the Wall led to *The Lost Border, The Landscape of the Iron Curtain*; and his study of Donald Trump's failed casino enterprises in Atlantic City resulted in *Atlantic City* (Circa Press, 2019). His photographs are held in the collections of the Museum of Modern Art and the Metropolitan Museum of Art.

First published in 2021 by Circa Press
Second edition published in 2025 ©2025 Circa Press Limited and Brian Rose

Circa Press
50 Great Portland Street
London W1W 7ND
www.circa.press

ISBN 978-1-911422-56-3

EU GPSR Authorised Representative:
Easy Access System Europe Oü, 16879218
Address: Mustamäe tee 50, 10621 Tallinn, Estonia
Email: gpsr@easproject.com Tel: +358 40 500 3575

Printed and bound in China

Cover design: April
Layout: Jean-Michel Dentand
Production: Dexter Premedia

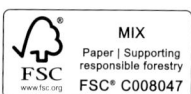